*Unravel
the messages
of your dreams
by learning
the meaning
of these
symbols:*

- Galloping horses
- Broken windows
- Spiders and snakes
- Friends and strangers
- Runaway automobiles
- Attics and alleys
- Wild animals...
  And many more

The Meaning of Your Dreams
was originally published by
Cornerstone Library.

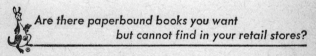

The Meaning of Your Dreams

by Valerie Moolman

PUBLISHED BY POCKET BOOKS NEW YORK

THE MEANING OF YOUR DREAMS

Cornerstone Library edition published February, 1969

Pocket Book edition published January, 1970

This *Pocket Book* edition includes every word
contained in the original, higher-priced edition. It is printed
from brand-new plates made from completely reset, clear, easy-to-read
type. *Pocket Book* editions are published by Pocket Books, a division
of Simon & Schuster, Inc., 630 Fifth Avenue, New York, N.Y. 10020.
Trademarks registered in the United States and other countries.

L

Contents

ONE

What's in a Dream?

Everybody Dreams

You've never had a dream in your life?

Everybody dreams.

It is too late now for anyone, any longer, to claim that he never dreams. It simply isn't even arguable any more.

Laboratory experiments have proved it. Surprised subjects, having sworn the night before that *they've* never had a dream in their lives, have been awakened time and time again in the middle of—guess what?—a dream, which they would then report with clarity and detail.

Most of the diehard "non-dreamers" are dreamers who forget their dreams rapidly and altogether. There are many factors affecting dream recall, but they all boil down to this: We do dream, and we do forget. Some people remember a number of their dreams very well indeed and others forget the whole lot altogether. Most of us are somewhere in between. It is not difficult to train ourselves to remember at least some of them. The first step is to realize that we have been forgetting them. Many "non-dreamers," having been advised that science says they definitely do dream, find themselves beginning to remember their dreams without any difficulty at all.

What Is a Dream?

During sleep the body relaxes and certain functions slow down but do not stop. We go on breathing, the heart beats, the blood flows . . . and the little cogwheels in the mind go right on turning. They are producing the sleep-thoughts that we call dreams.

The format of the dream is necessarily a little different from that of the waking-thought. With the conscious mind turned off, our use of language is restricted. We dream-think nonverbally, for the most part, which restricts both the presentation and the subject matter. Instead of articulating words, we see pictures. Instead of becoming aware of concepts or abstractions entering our heads, we see shapes symbolic of those thoughts appearing as if on a screen in front of us or on a stage around us. If an idea is incapable of presentation in this manner, with perhaps a little assist from sound or emotional coloring, we simply don't dream about it.

The pictures we see represent our thoughts; the symbols (in the form of people, creatures, houses, objects and so on) are representations of our abstract ideas or conceptions. Each dreamer creates his own story, plots it and peoples it; the emotions in it are his emotions. The actions, characters, feelings, colors, shadings, are all put there by him and *only* by him, although he will often call upon the most casual experiences of the day to shape the dream-stuff of the night. Even the least imaginative of us may have dreams that seem to be bizarre, yet are not. They have a superficial weirdness because we cannot readily untangle the symbolism and find out what it is that we are talking to ourselves about at night. The night thoughts are really hidden daytime thoughts brought out of hiding by our sleeping minds— and yet not brought *altogether* out of hiding or the shock of recognition might awaken us.

2

The thoughts that occupy us are not mere trivia, either. We do not dream of things for which we have absolutely no concern; we dream of deeply rooted problems, of secret wishes that demand fulfillment, or conflicts that matter to us very much. Even when a dream appears ridiculous—*particularly* then—it is a representation of something that is troubling us. Neither does it come simply to annoy; it parades the facts before our eyes and quite often offers solutions to the very problem it presents. (As a waking solution it is seldom practical, but that is a different story.)

Glorious Technicolor?

There still seems to be some discussion among sleep scientists as to the prevalence and importance of color in dreams. One prolonged study shows that most of us dream in monochrome most of the time, that about one dream in three has some color in it, that some people dream entirely in color, and that others never do. But the conclusions of the study are open to question: the subjects were not specifically asked about color. They volunteered their information.

Another study, involving eighty-seven dreams among thirty-eight subjects, indicated very strongly that people pay very little attention to color in dreams and simply fail to mention it unless queried. And when queried, these particular people answered, in tones of mild surprise, "What color was it? It was pink. How do I know it was pink? I saw it." Of this group of eighty-seven dreams (a small sampling, but indicative), only fifteen contained no specific reference to color, and there was no evidence that anything other than faulty observation or poor memory had anything to do with its absence. Chances are it was there, the dreamers took it for granted, and barely even noticed it. There is room for more

3

study in this direction, but at this stage it seems very likely that nearly all of us do dream in color more than we realize—simply because we *see* in color.

The presence of color in a dream does not necessarily reveal much about the dreamer, but the color may have significance if it is particularly noticeable in the dream, either because of its brightness, or its total absence in a situation demanding color, or the attention it calls to a particular object.

The Length of the Dream

We have all heard it said that dreams take place in the merest flash of time, and that aeons worth of action are packed into hectic seconds. This is true of a few dreams. It is also true that the mind is capable of condensing material and presenting enormous quantities of it to our attention simultaneously (as if in interlocking layers), which is one reason why some dreams seem so jumbled and difficult to sort out. But most dreams take a reasonable amount of time to unfold. It is also said that dreams per night are few and far between; maybe one or two, not more. There are more. Again, people think they dream but once or twice a night because they can't remember any more than the one or the couple experienced just before awakening. Current research shows that the average person goes through at least four or five dreaming periods per night, at eighty to ninety minute intervals, occupying a total of about 20 to 25 percent of the night's sleep.

The first of the night's dreams is usually fairly short, running in the neighborhood of five to ten minutes. As the night goes on the dream becomes longer, with perhaps the longest of the dreams lasting thirty to forty minutes and the average dream running about twenty minutes. So, far from taking place in a flash, most dreams unfold in about the same amount of time that they would take if acted out in waking life. The total dream period of the night is about an hour and a half to two hours. In fact, it is probably very much more than that, because there are other periods of nighttime mentation that occur in the deeper stages of sleep and have yet to be adequately studied.

Sometimes, each dream episode of a single night may be a chapter in a complete story, showing an almost logically plotted progression from step to step. Each new dream adds forward movement and a new idea, while at the same time shedding light on the preceding dreams. Or, sometimes, each dream or most dreams of the night might be a different version of exactly the same story—a story told by the dreamer to himself in different ways to make sure that he eventually gets the point. Each successive dream is thus a clear expression of the basic situation on the dreamer's mind; he is getting closer and closer to the heart of the matter.

(Sometimes the dreamer doesn't really care to understand himself at all, and throughout the night clothes his dream thoughts in such heavy disguises that he never sees through them. Sometimes, however, he uses the preliminary dreams to brace himself for the conclusion . . . and sometimes he actually enjoys the build-up if he knows the punch line is going to be good. If you follow for yourself the developing steps of a dream —that is, its progression within itself—or the progression of a series of dreams throughout the night or even over a period of nights, you often find that the dream scenes of a serialized dream story gets less and less abstract, and more and more explicit, as they unfold their tale. For example, what may appear in an early stage of a dream as a sensual plunge into a swimming pool may appear in a later stage as the sex act, unadorned.)

The Clash of Symbols

There is an apparently bizarre quality to many dreams, or at least in what we recall of them. They are fragmentary, disjointed, irrational, and, well, dreamlike. Part of their oddity lies in that faulty memory of ours; we remember only the fragments and forget the main theme and the transitional scenes. What made good sense at the time becomes nonsense in the light of day. Another, and probably the main, reason for the apparent weirdness of the dream is that the conscious mind is less accomplished at thinking in symbols than the sleeping mind, and has, in fact, less need to use them. The sleeping mind *does* distort our thoughts, and it does so largely because of its own limitations. (Its need to distort is something else again; there is no point in overemphasizing that aspect of symbolism, because most symbols can be deciphered, and quite easily, by the one who did the distorting in the first place—the dreamer himself.)

Abstract ideas, when they appear in dreams, literally appear; they manifest themselves in visible symbols that may initially be a puzzle to the waking mind but lend themselves fairly readily to interpretation. The sleeping mind has to use symbols to express abstract ideas, because the sleeping mind cannot "think" in abstractions. Objects, individuals (alive or dead), situations, concepts or perceptions of one kind or another that could easily be dealt with in abstract terms by the waking mind are translated into visual form in dream-thought; a thought that "comes to mind" when the mind is asleep comes in dressed to be *seen;* the dreamer's opinion or impression of something appears in picture form; and the sleeping mind, as economical as anything in nature, determines somewhere in its depths that as long as that

6

symbol is around anyway it might as well represent not just one idea but three or four or five. This kind of thing confuses the waking mind when it tries to recollect.

But we begin to realize, upon a little reflection, that we are quite well acquainted with symbolism and verbal shortcuts in our waking lives and in our speech. We use many symbols in waking life, and we use many symbolic expressions. Flags, emblems, road signs, traffic lights, warning sirens are among the most obvious of the symbols; we all use many more. The symbolism of our dreams is very similar—often it is exactly the same. We even use the same idiomatic or figurative expressions in dreams as we use in waking life. The only difference is that, in dreams, they are literally acted out. Such expressions as "wet blanket," "hit the ceiling," "down in the dumps," "bats in the belfry," "off his rocker," "wash my hands of it," "seeing red," "he's yellow," "fallen woman," "letting off steam," and dozens like them form the appropriate visual image in the dreams and may be interpreted accordingly.

When we have grasped this principle we are well on the way to cracking our own personal symbol code. It is more complex than our waking code, of course, but the waking code provides us with a solid foundation.

Typical Dreams

We are all very different, and we all have our individual thoughts and even our individual symbols, but all the same a major study has revealed that certain dreams are common to many, many people and lend themselves to a fairly standard interpretation no matter who is dreaming them. These are the dreams:

Exhibition dreams, in which varying degrees of nudity are to be found; dreams of an openly sexual nature;

7

flying and floating dreams; falling, or clinging-to-the-edge-of-a-precipice dreams; dreams of the death of self or others; loss-of-tooth dreams; examination dreams; missing train-or-bus dreams; dreams of running away from someone or something; glued-to-the spot dreams; dreams of crawling through a tunnel or other confined, narrow space; dreams of driving or riding in a moving vehicle; swimming, water, and sporting-on-the-beach dreams; dreams of fighting or quarreling; dreams of gambling; dreams of climbing stairs or mountains; dreams of moving around inside a house or other building; dreams of being imprisoned; dreams of encountering an officer of the law; and dreams of hurting someone or being hurt.

The fact that there are such things as "typical dreams" and "standard interpretations" in no way diminishes our individual differences. It points them up, even while pointing out that the human experience is something shared and that in general outlines we are not outlandishly different from each other. The standard interpretation of a typical dream may be perfectly valid, but it gives us no more than a foundation upon which to build the intricate details that make up the interpretation of the dreams of any individual. One dream of falling or losing a tooth or running upstairs isn't going to tell anybody anything about himself unless he is able to relate it immediately to an immediate experience. Typical dreams do not tell us much about the dreamer unless they are accompanied by a strong emotional reaction, or unless they are repeated in one guise or another over a period of time or at least throughout the course of a dream series. Dreams and dream symbols, typical or otherwise, must be examined in relation to a whole picture consisting of the dreamer himself, his own associations to the dream, and his other dreams.

If, after scrutiny, we see a repetition of certain ideas in the form of symbols, we can begin to regard them as meaningful messages. When the same dream and/or the same symbol recurs again and again, we *know* it must have meaning. Superficial interpretation is easy—but what does it really mean, in practical terms, to the dreamer? This is where the real work begins. In the light of the standard interpretation, what does the dreamer have to say about his own dreams? How did he feel during the dream? How does he feel about it afterwards? Why should he feel guilt, or shame, or whatever it is? What does the symbolic action or object remind him of? How does he feel when thus reminded?

It soon becomes clear that even "typical" dreams are not so obvious as they might seem at first. The dreamer makes use of available symbols to express what he has in his mind; the symbols do not make use of him. If the dreams of all of us are superficially similar, we cannot therefore assume that their message to each one of us, with our own particular needs and problems, is the same. The true, the pointed, significance of each dream is individual to the dreamer.

In addition to the imagery we share with so many hundreds of thousands of other dreamers, we each have certain favorite symbols that we use in dreams just as we have certain favorite expressions or habits of speech in waking life. The richness of our dream vocabulary is our own. Some special images are our own. So is some of our language. "Baby," "honey," "peach," "rat," "pig," "cow," "bag," "fruit," "nuts," are only a few samples of the many words that have different meanings for different people. These differences must be taken into account when any attempt is being made to interpret dreams.

Content

Symbolism notwithstanding, most dreams are not particularly fantastic or exciting. Fleeting memory tells us that we have been attending a theater of the absurd, but as we recall the main ingredients of the dream it usually becomes apparent that there wasn't anything too special about it. Few dreams take place in exotic settings. The merest minority include glamorous, well-known personalities or really dramatic occurrences. Events of major national or international importance are seldom repeated in dreams. Gorgeous actresses, tropical isles, space ships, and fantasies of heroism are exceptions rather than the rule.

What *do* we dream of? Of our own immediate little world and the people in it. Pretty humdrum material, for the most part. The scenes may be dolled up and distorted, and quite often the disguises are so good that we don't recognize ourselves or our wives or husbands or our homes, but when the disguise is penetrated we're right back in a situation taken straight from waking life . . . a conflict going back to an hour before bedtime, or twenty, thirty years before. With a little unraveling it can be seen that almost every dream is a neatly plotted little story told with an economy of phrase and action, featuring a few basic characters who can be quite easily identified when they have shed their guise as strangers.

Perhaps it should be stressed here that no unpleasant dream-thought or projection is anything but an observation of our own making. What we dream about other people is not their doing; it is ours. It may have some basis in fact—for, after all, we have insights in our sleeping as well as in our waking thoughts—but it is strongly colored and shaped by our own opinions, our own fears, our own wishes, our own prejudices. Just because you dream that someone is madly in love with you doesn't mean you should rush out and buy the ring; it means that you dream-plotted a story to gratify yourself.

The Nature of the Nightmare

Nightmares are the most common of dream disturbances; we all have them at some time or another. One major study showed that, in young adults, two out of five dreams can be expected to contain sequences of fear; and another reported that two out of three dreams tend to be unpleasant. This should be easy enough to understand if we accept the proposition that one of the main reasons for dreaming is to work out our conflicts. The conflict isn't much fun to begin with, but if it becomes too great, or if we come too close to seeing the worst of ourselves too clearly, the dream awakens us and we say that we have had a nightmare. We also use our own control over the dream to punish ourselves for something our conscience tells us we shouldn't have done; feeling that we deserve to suffer, we give ourselves a nightmare.

Workings of the Night-Mind

Our dreaming minds have an advantage over our waking minds in that they are free from the bombardment of impressions, the continual action, the endless stimuli and the various other demands of the external world. Left to itself, and closed to the outside world, the sleeping mind has a time of respite in which it can dwell on certain ideas without intrusion. It even has an opportunity to do creative work, linking ideas together in combinations that tend to be overlooked by the waking mind. Bypassing the usual daytime clutter, it matches ideas together in new ways, coordinates thoughts from

11

here and there, comes up with different combinations, reaches new insights—and quite often achieves what we call "inspiration."

Robert Louis Stevenson dreamed his plots, and later sold them. Samuel Taylor Coleridge received his vision of Xanadu in a dream, and in that dream composed the *Kubla Khan* that he could only half remember upon waking. Organic chemist Friedrich A. Kekulé, wondering about the likely arrangement of atoms within a molecule of benzene, dreamed of a snake with its tail in its mouth and awoke to the "inspiration" of the benzene ring. It was in a dream that Elias Howe solved his problem about the right kind of needle to use (with the eye in the sharp end) in his just-about-to-be-invented sewing machine. William Makepeace Thackeray, sleeping, dreamed a title for his novel about Becky Sharp, and convinced his publisher that *Vanity Fair* had a salable sound about it. There are many such cases, some of them quite dazzling; so many of them, and so dazzling, that we are tempted to think there is something magical or mystical about them. And it is true that some night insights, some dream messages, are very hard to explain.

Yet most of them are readily explainable in terms of the hardworking human mind, busily sorting out, assessing, and coordinating facts and fancies in the dreamer's dreams.

The Question of Prophecy

If there is any truth to the idea that dreams do or can prophesy the future then we must radically revise our views on free will, predetermination, and the nature of time.

We may have to.

From Biblical times until today and no doubt until

tomorrow and tomorrow and tomorrow, dreams have been regarded by some as having prophetic value. A housewife dreams a name, a number, or a letter the night before the running of the Derby. The next day, predictably, she backs the winning horse. A construction worker hears a number in his dreams, and wins the lottery. A mother dreams her child is ill, and next day the little one has a fever. A busnessman dreams that an ocean liner upon which he has booked passage is floating upside down in the lonely sea. He cancels, and the postscript to this story is the sinking of the Titanic. A traveling salesman dreams of a hotel fire and changes his hotel reservations; the hotel he did not stay in burns down. An executive dreams of a plane crash and postpones his other-city appointment. The plane does crash. A secretary dreams that she is going to get fired, and lo and behold——

The most famous predictive dream on record is that of Abraham Lincoln. A few days before his assassination, it is said, he dreamed he heard weeping and saw, in the East Room of the White House, a soldier or soldiers standing guard over a corpse on a catafalque. Upon asking, "Who is dead in the White House?" he was told, "The President. He was killed by an assassin."

This story has curdled blood since it was first told, but it should not be regarded as in any way unusual because premonitory dreams and visions of disaster are very common indeed. They can often—though not always—be easily explained. Lincoln, for instance, was the recipient of much hate-mail and many threats on his life. He knew that there had been plots against him that had failed, and that there might be one that would not fail. He knew that there were diehards who wished him dead and were doing more than wishing. He had every reason to suppose that his life was in danger, because it was. His dream, then, was not so much a

13

vision of the future as the contemplation of a likelihood with its roots planted firmly in the past and present.

Similarly, the mother who predicts her child's illness is less prognosticator than typical mother. She knows her child, senses changes in him, and she worries. That her worries prove to be justified is scarcely magic at all. And, of course, the secretary who predicts her loss of job is at least unconsciously and probably consciously aware that she is doing a bad job and deserves to lose it. The ship that went down . . . the hotel that burned . . . the plane that crashed. . . . How many people dreamed of a happy voyage, a pleasant stay, a safe flight? Impossible, of course, to even guess; but there must have been such dreams, and they were wrong.

Other apparently prophetic dreams can sometimes be explained in terms of wish-fulfillment. We dream certain dreams as a substitute for reality, but we dream others because we are looking forward to a future reality. Hopefully, we dream of something that we want, of a natural, daytime-fulfillable desire. That we sometimes actually get what we want is not so strange; if we want something enough to dream about it as a *fait accompli,* we want it enough to do something about getting it and making that dream come true.

Lucky Numbers

Many of today's so-called Dream Books are published for the benefit of policy players, who look for lucky numbers wherever they can find them. They find them in such books as the *Prince Ali Lucky Five Star Dream Book* and *Old Aunt Dinah's Policy Players Sure Guide to Lucky Dreams and Lucky Numbers* and a host of others with similar names. These little books have a certain charm about them, and once in a great while their dream interpretations—or definitions, rath-

14

er—do land, in a blind, coincidental way, somewhere near the truth. Maybe their numbers do, too, because once in a while, of course, a dream number will pay off for somebody. The great Zolar himself comments on this as follows:

"Many persons have written me about various sums of money they have won from time to time with the aid of their dream numbers. Personally I believe that in most cases coincidence played the major part in their good fortune. It has been my experience that Lady Luck is very unpredictable and that in the long run, except in very rare cases, persons lose much more than they win in this form of speculation. Because there are always exceptions to the rules, and due to the popular demand, I reduce all my dream interpretations into number vibrations."

No numbers mentioned in the following pages have any discernible vibrations, although they may have meaning.

Wilhelm Stekel had a patient who dreamed numbers and, on rare occasions, won on them, which naturally sold her on the idea of pulling lucky numbers out of dreams. Stekel managed, in analysis, to evoke from her certain associations to those numbers (ages, dates, and so on) that led him to interpretations which had nothing whatsoever to do with luck or lotteries or the ponies. But why did her dream numbers prove out on any occasion at all? "I think there is a very simple explanation why these numbers proved winners," Stekel said. "She dreams of them every night, and in her street, after every drawing, she looks into the window of a lotto agency to see which numbers have won. Her winning numbers cannot fail to turn up or come out occasionally. Of course she 'counts the hits and forgets the misses.' " Or, as Voltaire put it, "Dreams which have come to pass are always predictions which no one can doubt, no account being taken of dreams which are never fulfilled. One dream accomplished has more effect than 100 which fail."

But. . . . Numbers and coincidences aside, there *are* predictive dreams that totally defy explanation in what we like to think of as "logical" terms. There is a growing body of evidence that strongly suggests that some dreams of some people may truly predict the future. There is not yet enough evidence; such evidence as there is cannot be regarded as unassailable proof; no definitive scientific study, with test control conditions, has yet been undertaken to determine the authenticity and accuracy of predictive dreams. Until there are such studies, there will be sceptics. But, in the meantime, how are we to explain a man like Edgar Cayce, for example, a relatively untutored man whose sleeping mind was a storehouse of knowledge about present, past, and future, and whose dream-predictions of decades ago—in regard to both trivial and cataclysmic events—have been coming true and are coming true with awesome accuracy? *Is* there a universal, a collective unconscious that we—or some of us—are capable of tapping with our own unconscious? Do we so thoroughly misunderstand the nature of time that even to speak of "prediction" is to err—because the future already exists somewhere, somehow, on some unimaginable plane . . . ?

What is evident as we survey the pooled ignorance of all the experts is that some dreams cannot be explained unless we admit them to be predictions, and that the vast majority of dreams that appear to be prophetic are nothing of the sort.

For our own purposes we can generally assume that the average person's "prophetic" dreams are usually forecasts that have a reasonable hope of coming true. Past and present tell us what the future probabilities are, and thus in our own predictive dreams we are usually projecting our own future so that we can have a preview of it. Obviously, the sleeping mind has much data on which to base a prophecy. This is surely true especially in relation to problem situations and decisions. According to Dr. Alfred Adler, dreams reflect unsolved problems and are rehearsals of their possible solutions or of the dreamer's future actions in connection with that problem. Thus, if a dreamer dreams of five different courses of action, or five different ways of solving a problem, and then sees one of them coming true———! It's instant prophecy, and he's quite impressed with himself, forgetting all about the four trial balloons that went off in the wrong directions. And he also forgets, if he ever gave it a thought, that his inspirational forecast was a product of a mind that, undistracted by swarms of external stimuli, was able to concentrate on the facts, coordinate them, sort them out, and suggest probabilities to itself.

Scientific exploration and explanation of the dream process and of dreams themselves have come far within the last few decades. There is still a long way to go, a lot to find out, a lot to explain. But this we do know: We need our dreams for our physical and mental health, and we need our full quota of them.

The practical value of dream study and dream analysis is not that it gives us a chance to peer into the future to pick a winning horse, but to figure ourselves out and make changes as suggested by the insights we receive. In this way we can and do affect our future, even if our dream revelations have been commonsense messages from us to us rather than prophecies—not so much predictions, as advice.

TWO

Interpretation: Why and How

"The generality of mankind do not give much credit to Dreams, yet, considering that many strange accidents have been foretold by them, many mischiefs prevented, and many wickednesses detected, it may not be amiss to set down here what experience has observed concerning them. A dream is a motion or fiction of the soul, signifying either good or evil to come, and it dependeth on the character or class as to whether it may signify its true meaning or directly the contrary."

For the foregoing observations we are indebted to Aunt Dinah, patroness of the policy players, and though we cannot find ourselves in full agreement with her we do recognize the echo of truth in what she says. If we look closely at our dreams we may well find it possible to prevent "strange accidents" and "mischiefs," and almost without doubt we will find "wickednesses" within ourselves that lend themselves to correction. It is also a fact that we must pay much attention to "character or class" of a dream before accepting it at face value, because a dream of happiness *may* be the wish-fulfillment device of a desperately unhappy soul and a dream in which fear is dominant *may* actually be telling a story of consuming desire. At this stage, though, we must depart from Dinah. Dreams are not fiction; and though some of them may be speculative looks into the future, *none* of them are omens of either good or evil. They are the creations of our own minds, and an attempt to understand them should not be put on a par with teacup reading or fortune telling through some random arrangement of playing cards.

The majority of our dream thoughts are of value not as reminders of what not to eat just before going to bed, not as predictions for the fourth at Aqueduct, not as warnings against tall dark strangers, not as route maps to the pot of gold at the foot of the rainbow, but as keys to what makes us tick. In our dreams we express what we think about ourselves, our associates, our loved ones, our inner conflicts, and the world around us; we reveal—if we could only remember!—how we conceive of our own impulses; we make admissions to ourselves that we cannot bring ourselves to make during our waking lives. These admissions are not always direct, or readily recognizable, partly because of the limitations of the dream language and partly because even in dreams we cannot quite face some of our own thoughts and conceptions, but a little digging strips away the various disguises and shows what the dreamer is really thinking of.

Thus the interpretation of dreams is the device whereby we unlock the door to the hidden compartments of the mind and discover what problems and conflicts lie beneath the surface. In waking life we are only, as a rule, aware of the superficial and obvious problems of our waking days. In our sleeping life we delve beneath the obvious and seek out the reality of ourselves. So deep do we go that upon surfacing again we cannot bring back with us the meaning we have seen, and therefore we have to make an effort to piece together whatever we do remember.

But is it worth it? Surely it must be, to anyone who

cares about the nature of the human being, to anyone who cares to understand himself. Surely it must be, to anyone who wonders about the cause of some unnamed, difficult-to-pinpoint-or-explain anxiety—which, in all likelihood, has its roots in some long-forgotten experience that no longer matters at all. Deep down within us we build up conflicts that get worse and worse because we do not face them . . . though many of them are relatively trivial to begin with. Before we can solve those inner conflicts we have to bring them to light and look them in the eye. We may not be particularly delighted with what we see, but often the light of understanding shows them to be midgets rather than monsters; and once we have looked them in the eye and seen them shrink we find ourselves better able to function effectively and deal rationally with the challenges of daily life. (It's as if we were to say, "Good grief, is *that* what I was worrying about!" and then feel a load falling from our shoulders.) And even if the problems or conflict situations do not automatically shrink upon exposure to the light of day, at least we have given ourselves a chance to size them up, define them, and take steps to consciously solve whatever it is that ails us.

We look into a dream and see much that we do not know in the top part of our minds; we look into a dream, and we explore it, and we discover much that we would not otherwise have known about ourselves. We piece the parts together and gradually we begin to understand what we think about our own motives and acts and impulses, and what we think about our environment and the people in it. Gradually we extend our knowledge of ourselves. We gaze at thoughts and concepts that we might prefer to ignore, but in the gazing we gain insight; we glimpse truths, and in the glimpsing we sometimes find an inner peace and sometimes a view of the right direction to take in our daily doings.

Through self-understanding we can make adjustments, changes, improvements in our own behavior, or at least we can accept ourselves more freely; and through self-understanding we reach a greater degree of understanding and empathy for others.

Probably the major difficulty in interpreting dreams is their elusiveness; we can't do much interpreting if we can't remember. Actually, it is possible to get into the habit of paying attention to dreams and remembering them better afterwards. The more we think about dreaming and the harder we try to catch the dream-wisp before it disappears altogether, the more often we succeed in recapturing the fragments and the easier it becomes to remember.

There are two things we can do to aid recall: (1) Upon waking, keep the eyes closed and lie very still in a loose, relaxed way; let the mind reach back to catch whatever dream fragments are still floating near the surface before any movement or outer distraction has a chance to drown them altogether. (2) Immediately upon opening the eyes, write down everything that is remembered—every whole dream, every part dream, every fragment, every wisp, every scene, every word, every character, every creature, every color.

Even when remembering has become a habit, the notes serve as a permanent record of things dreamed; over a period of time they begin to form a pattern that is really a picture of ourselves.

There are a number of points that should be born in mind by anyone who wants to delve into the meaning of his dreams:

1. There are no universal rules in dream interpretation, just as there is no rigid set of universal symbols. Sometimes a methodical plodding through the memory banks is less successful than the unrestrained, free-associative leap; and sometimes that free-associative leap

lands one on a pile of fantasy. Probably the best we can do is steer a careful course between extremes. As for dream symbols, the symbols listed in the following pages are those which appear frequently in the dreams of countless people and have been found to express the meanings attributed to them. They may have many other meanings for many other dreamers. That does not, however, make them invalid as guides; the fact that they are similarly employed by a great many people is a fair indication that they may be similarly employed by a great many *other* people; further, anyone seeing what they mean to some dreamers can usually figure out what *else* they can mean. Anyone wanting to discover what a dream symbol means to himself, specifically, must honestly bring his own associations to bear; he must dig into his memory and conscience and be ready to face what he finds; he must be able to "confess" to himself certain aspects of his personality, character, and past life, and use these confessions to shed new light on the symbols employed in his dreams.

2. A fast, glib look at one or two symbols is *not* dream interpretation. Every remembered aspect of the dream must be scrutinized, from main to subsidiary characters, from giants to insects, from action to immobility, from participation to observation, from scenic backdrop to small object in the foreground, from emotional coloring to lack of it; and then the *whole picture* must be viewed in the light of what it can mean to the dreamer himself rather than what it appears to mean after a fast glance at the pages of a dream-book glossary. No symbol has any meaning in itself. No single symbol carries the full meaning of a dream. No group of symbols has any meaning in a vacuum. There is no meaning *per se* in symbols and no point in seizing upon possible meaning unless an honest attempt is made to

relate the symbolism to the facts of the dreamer's life and personality.

3. Any dream symbol may, and often does, carry more than one idea at the same time; for example, one person seen in a dream may be a condensation of two or more actual people. Any dream idea may be split into several parts—for instance, into several people—that represent different and probably conflicting aspects of an individual or situation.

4. Dream actions that are repeated again and again relate to specific and important problems. The repetition indicates the dreamer's wish to solve his problems *and* his lack of success in doing so. By the same token, any repetition of ideas, in whatever symbolic clothing they may wear, points up the importance of those ideas to the dreamer. Dreams that recur throughout the years usually express the main theme of the dreamer's life.

5. Any nonsense in a dream, even a nonsensical word or phrase, may be suspected of carrying a meaning that is not nonsensical at all; it may camouflage the most important idea of the dream. Ridiculous dream actions or illogical behavior on the part of any of the characters demand close inspection by the dream student. A dream that is so bizarre that it apparently "doesn't make any sense" may make a great deal of sense by the time it has been analyzed.

6. The central idea or theme of the dream usually carries the problem that is of main concern to the dreamer.

7. There is some meaning to all our dreams, but that does not mean all dreams are equally meaningful. Although it is of value to get into the habit of noting every dream and every dream-fragment, it is *not* of value to try to interpret every stray night-thought as if it were a momentous message. The purpose of keeping a dream record is first to prod the memory and then to

provide oneself with an overall view of what patterns are building up, what ideas are repeated, and what dream aspects have the greatest emotional impact. It is possible, after a while, to separate the wheat from the chaff, and to focus on the main themes or on apparently isolated dreams that seem to hold a particularly compelling interest for the dreamer. In all likelihood even these apparent one-shot dreams are part of a series.

8. One dream tells us very little about ourselves. If we really want to know enough about our inner selves to gain practical help in our waking lives, we have to patiently collect a great many dreams and try to pinpoint the central idea of each—and then see if that is not also the central theme of an entire series. The theme of a chain of dreams gives us the full story of what weighs upon our sleeping minds, and the details of some of the dreams tend to fill in what is missing from the others. Sometimes the dreams of a single night are much like the chapters of a book, with each dream-chapter building on and adding significance to the ones before. Sometimes a dream pattern experienced over a period of time turns out, upon scrutiny, to be a kind of serialization of one particularly significant story or conflict theme. The central idea may be disguised in various ways, so that the unity of the dream series is not at first apparent; therefore the self-analyst must bear in mind that any idea can be expressed in many different ways and by many different symbols instead of leaping to the conclusion that he has a wide and wild variety of dreams. He probably doesn't; he's just being fooled by their disguises. A dream that at first seems difficult to understand is, quite often, little more than a repetition of the old main theme and may be interpreted with the help of previous dreams.

Steps in Interpretation

1. Determine within yourself that you are going to remember your dreams, and remind yourself of this resolve every night when turning off the light.

2. Upon awaking, keep the eyes closed and lie still; let the mind roam about and recapture all it can. Fasten on all wisps of dream clues and track them down.

3. Now, before the fleeting thoughts begin to get away again, quickly write them down. Include the main theme, the characters, the action, the extras, any animals or other creatures, the general setting, the furnishings or other inanimate objects, the objects actually used, the way they were used, the emotional coloring— everything you can possibly think of. In parenthesis, add whatever associative thoughts happen to come immediately to mind.

4. Later in the day, at a leisure hour, read carefully through your notes until you have them all in mind. Relax in a comfortable chair, put your feet up, and think over what you have read. Taking one dream at a time, break each dream down to a simple outline; try to reduce it to what it seems to be saying. Note the points that stand out as apparently important, nonsensical, weird, frightening, and so on.

5. Take a long, slow look at the apparent overall meaning. Is it so obvious that you can spot it right away? It's possible. If not, what comes into your mind when you think about the central idea? What does it remind you of? What does it mean to you? Nothing, perhaps. Maybe much more is needed before you begin to see the glimmerings of an idea. But possibly—just possibly—you get a tiny clue.

6. With or without your clue, dissect the dream into its various components. Look up the dream symbols and see what they have meant to many thousands of other

people. Can they have a similar meaning for you? If so, what is it? If not—if not, are you sure you're not kidding yourself? Have another look, and think again. What are your own private associations to the stuff of the dream? What do those dream thoughts suggest to your waking mind?

7. Fit the dream details back into the overall picture and see what you have now. Have you been honest about how you felt in the dream? About how you feel now that you are looking at it from the outside? Have any memories been jogged, or can you jog them now? What comes into your mind when you review the elements and the whole? Does anything in the dream remind you, no matter how peripherally, of anything in your life? Or of any part of any other dream? Are you letting your ideas loose, or are you restraining them? Let them flow freely—have a private brainstorming session. If some of your associations get out of hand and go beyond the meaning of the dream, practice and other dreams will help to get you back on the right path.

8. Look at your other dreams in the same way; dreams from the same night, and dreams from other nights. Look at other dreams in the light of the knowledge gained from any one, and look at any and every one in the light of the knowledge gained from interpretation of others. Certainly, not all dreams will turn out to be part of a series, but there is a kind of consistency to nearly all the dreams of any single dreamer—even though, on the surface, they may seem wildly different. Just as we seldom do anything that is totally contrary to our nature, so do we seldom dream anything that does not fit into a basic pattern. Try to look at the individual dreams, therefore, as though they might be part of some larger pattern. Even if they are not part of some night-time serial they are still part of the pattern that is you

. . . and the unlocking of a single dream may lead to the unlocking of many.

You won't have the professional analysts shaking in their boots, but you will come to something more of self-understanding and probably more tolerance for others—and you may be led through these pages and your own efforts to a much deeper study of your dreams, yours fears, your longings, and yourself.

THREE

Strangers, Friends, and Selves

We seem to dream about a lot of people, many of them strangers. Actually, we don't. If there is such a thing as an "average dream," it is likely to be populated by no more than three to five people. In many cases the dreamer himself is at least two or three of these "other" people. In crowd scenes, when they occur, the onlookers usually represent a feeling (I-really-shouldn't-be-doing-this-at-all-What-would-other-people-think?) on the part of the dreamer, which in turn represents his conception of public opinion.

Each of us is the main character in his own dream, whether we are onlooker or activist. If the dreamer's waking tendency is to look on at life as if at a passing show, then in dreams he also tends to be the onlooker. If he leads an active life, then in dreams he tends to participate quite actively. If he conceives of himself as a timid, joyless person, then in dreams he may be just as timid and joyless—or he may be lively, jolly, and full of fun, thus fulfilling his deeply hidden wish to be a different kind of person.

If a dreamer conceives of himself as having several different, conflicting characteristics, then in his dreams he may represent himself in the form of several different people—one, perhaps gentle and loving, another timo-

28

rous, another bubbling with overflowing rage. Aspects of himself may appear in the forms of animals, or of other people whom he does not know . . . or thinks he doesn't.

We do not dream about people we don't know, even if the faces we see are those of strangers. We dream about people we *do* know, and what we think of them, and what we think of ourselves. We dream of people who matter to us or who stand for some idea that we share. When we dream, as we rarely do, of prominent people in the news, it may occasionally mean that they interest us in some personal way but more often that something about them represents or symbolizes something to us. People who mean nothing to us, people about whom we have no conflicting feelings, do not appear in our dreams. We dream about the people who are close to us and with whom we still have something to resolve; and we do not recognize them easily, or perhaps at all, in their guise of a teacher, movie star, ship's captain, gentle stranger, faceless tormentor, or misty figure from our past.

Youngsters dream of father, mother, brothers, sisters, sometimes other close relatives, and occasionally school friends. Adults dream more often of husband, wife, lover(s), and children, though in many adult dreams parental figures and grown siblings play strong parts. When they do, it usually means that the conflicts of their youth have been unsolved and still are raging in the backyards of the mind.

Individuals whom we know and love may appear with monstrous characteristics. We tend to think, on wakening, that we have received a revelation about their character, but in this we are wrong. In some cases, it is true, we may have received a dream-insight into the true nature of a supposed loved one or close associate, but the chances are much greater that we—for it

29

is our dream, not theirs—have imputed characteristics to them based on our own doubts and fears and guilts and misconceptions.

Now, about those mysterious strangers. . . .

Let it be remembered that a dream makes pictures out of many kinds of thoughts, including abstractions. A thought thus pops into the mind in a certain shape, though the original thought has no "shape" at all. What shape does it take? The shape of fear, perhaps—a featureless pursuer. The shape of memory—a departed loved one, come alive. A feeling of helplessness—a baby. What baby? Why, the dreamer himself!

Often, that stranger is a concept of some sort. Often, the stranger represents some part of ourselves that we don't know too well, or decline to recognize with the waking mind. Often, the stranger is the personification of some facet of someone we know. Often, the stranger represents something that we are unsure of—strange thoughts, perhaps, taking the shape of a strange person.

Then there is the not-quite-stranger. Now you know him, now you don't. The face is familiar . . . and all at once it isn't. Who is he? He is a person about whom you have mixed feelings; even yourself, perhaps. Or not a person at all, but a train of thought expressed in picture form. Or it becomes clear in mid-dream that the face is not exactly familiar *or* strange, but the face of someone casually met and unimportant to you. The candy store man, for example; what is he to you and why should you dream of him? Well, he may be your secret passion; but more likely he clicks off a reminder of things past, or something about him or his candy store represents something of significance to you in a present conflict situation, or some aspect of the man reminds you of some aspect of yourself or someone else.

Strangers they may seem, but strangers they are not. They have come (because you sent for them) to tell you something about you. Only *you* can figure out what it may be. And only you can know what feelings you have in your dream about that mean little brother, loving father, helpless child, pursuer, neighborhood merchant, old flame, or faceless figure. . . .

Actor (Actress)—In dreams involving actor images the dreamer may play the part of the star (it is almost bound to be a star; the dream actor is seldom second lead or extra) or he may assign that role to someone else. The dreamer who casts himself as actor reveals his wish to enjoy the limelight, the glamor, the fame, and possibly the exciting sex life presumed to be enjoyed by those dazzling beings of stage and celluloid and TV tube. As an occasional dream it may represent no more than a fleeting thought, inspired by the day's doings and possibly colored by an evening at the movies, and as such it represents little more than a brief upsurge of envy and self-gratification. However, if such a dream recurs with any frequency, the dreamer should begin to ask himself why he chooses to be an unreal person living in an unreal world. Perhaps he is finding it increasingly difficult to face up to the life that he knows and has found a way to escape reality by assuming a glamorous new personality.

When the dreamer retains his own identity and dreams of someone else as actor, he is probably indicating his envy of that person and possibly his admiration or respect for him as an interesting, glamorous, and popular individual. There is a slight possibility that he feels genuine admiration for the actual star, but it is more likely that he has given the role of actor to one of his own close associates and himself provided the Rock Hudson mask to reveal his conception of that individual. On the other hand, the dreamer may not be dreaming of individuals at all but of ideas and desires. If he meets actors in his dreams he may be revealing his wish to associate with more exciting people than those who make up his present circle of acquaintances and friends.

When the non-star dreamer develops his dream plot, working in a personal encounter with this star of his own creation, he gives away even more about himself. If he is somehow bested or humiliated in the confrontation, he is reflecting his own poor opinion of his qualities and capabilities. But if he comes out on top, he is either indulging in wish-fulfillment or showing himself to have a pretty healthy self-image.

Adam—The old Adam does sometimes appear in dreams, and what he means depends, as always, on the dreamer's own associations. If, in waking life, he thinks of "the old Adam" as the Devil within one, why, then, that's what he thinks in dreams. Or perhaps the dreamer knows, or has read extensively about, an Adam in his waking life, and that real Adam has a personal significance. Otherwise, the dream-Adam represents the dreamer's father . . . first man in the world, first in the hearts of his children.

Admiral—Sea captain will do just as well, and more people are inclined to dream about captains than admirals because more captains than admirals are likely to be encountered in life. However, the admiral has the rank and thus commands the more respect.

Generally, any uniformed, authoritative figure is in dreams a figure of authority and power. That figure may symbolize father, command, or even God.

Specifically, an admiral or other high-ranking naval officer represents a figure capable of commanding at sea, one who is able to take the helm and navigate successfully through the sea of life. Anyone aboard with him is in safe hands.

One who dreams of being an admiral is one who either feels capable of command and secure in the belief that he is master of himself—or wishes that he did. Whichever cap fits, wear it, as the saying goes.

When a woman dreams of an admiral figure she is expressing her inner belief that the man thus symbolized is masterful and dependable. She may wish to be dependent upon him and let him guide the ship, but at the same time she may feel some sense of inferiority or fear. Very likely her feelings are mixed, as are a child's feelings toward a father. When a man dreams of an admiral figure other than himself he is revealing his own feelings of insecurity and his need to depend on someone else. He may already be leaning on a father figure, or he may be wishing that he could. If the admiral of his dream represents a specific individual rather than a symbol of authority and strength, the dreamer is revealing his awe of the man or his dependence upon him.

Angel—An angel in a dream may represent the higher self of the dreamer or a spiritual force in his life. The appearance of such a being, which is none too common, may be indicative of a wish to possess those qualities we attribute to angels—the qualities of gentleness, of love, of mercy, of purity, and of forgiveness. Sometimes the dream angel is symbolic of an individual to whom we attribute those same qualities. Or the angel may represent the dreamer's fear of, or wish for, death. The emotion accompanying the dream is the main key to interpretation.

Baby—Dream babies are common and complex symbols that mean many things to many people. To dreamers of spiritual inclination, a dream baby may represent a rebirth of the self to a new awareness or higher ideals. The growing baby, in these terms, is a struggle toward perfection of the spiritual or higher self, while a sickly baby may indicate failure to overcome the baser ideas or worldly obstacles that obstruct the path toward spiritual realization.

More often, the dream baby is a less spiritual symbol of the dreamer's feelings, wishes, hopes, and fears.

A parent who dreams of a baby or babies may be symbol-thinking of his love for his own children, but at the same time he may be identifying himself with his child and thus revealing his own feeling of childlike helplessness and/or his wish to be loved and pampered without having to give anything in return. He may have the hidden desire to be without responsibilities at all.

A childless adult who often dreams of babies may be expressing one or more of a multitude of feelings. He could be wishing for a child. He could be wishing that he could return to the days of his babyhood when his parents loved and looked after him and carried the load of everyday responsibilities that he now has. (It must be remembered, in dream interpretation, that when a dreamer "sees" an individual outside of himself, whether that individual be baby, adult, gentleman or thief, follower or leader, he is often seeing some aspect of himself. And there is some baby in the most mature of us.) He, or she, might have the hidden thought that he has acted like a baby; or that a loved one, or close associate, is behaving like a child.

When women, childless or otherwise, dream of babies or of having a baby they may be expressing their wish to have a child or their fear of pregnancy. In some dreams it is apparent that the dreamer is stirred by maternal feelings even while dreading the thought of giving birth. Sometimes the baby dream may be indicative of the dreamer's desire for a more satisfactory sexual life or a need to prove her womanliness.

Elderly people may, in their dreams of babies, be revealing a long-buried yearning to be young parents once again—or perhaps not even parents, but young adults of child-bearing age.

Children who dream of babies may be hugging their feelings of neglect to themselves and wishing that they could return to the days when they were nursed and cuddled instead of being told to get their hands out of the cookie jar and keep out from underfoot. If they have a younger sister or brother, their baby dreams often indicate jealousy of the newcomer, even though that "newcomer" may have outgrown the baby stage. The younger sibling is still the baby of the family and the older child resents being displaced from his mother's arms. He may dream of being back in those warm arms; he may dream of watching from the sidelines while mother lavishes love on the intruder, or he may dream wishfully of something happening to the other child. When such dreams persist through the teen-age years and into young adulthood, it is apparent that the feeling of resentment is quite strong and that the young dreamer is too dependent on the exclusive love of his parents. (See also Child, Children)

Banker—A dream of a banker may be a direct translation of a daytime encounter with a bank official or a problem of financial security. If no such obvious interpretation is possible, the dreamer may be expressing his diffidence in dealing with powerful business associates and his lack of confidence in his own handling of affairs. The banker deals in something of much value; to the dreamer it may be "love," possibly "power," possibly the coin-that-can-buy-all-things *including* love, power, prestige, authority, or whatever the dreamer wants most.

As guardian over these vast resources, the banker himself is a figure of power. If the dreamer sees himself

35

as the banker he is either envisioning himself as prestigious and powerful or he is revealing his wish to be prestigious and powerful. If another figure in the dreamer's playlet is the banker, then the dreamer is expressing his respect and admiration for that figure . . . who may in turn represent the father-figure who is capable of giving all things and withholding all things, primarily love. When the dream banker is apparently identifiable as a real-life friend, the dreamer reveals his affection and esteem for that friend; when the banker is something less than a friend—possibly an unpleasant associate or even an enemy—then the dreamer is expressing his awe and possibly fear of the individual. If the dreamer should dream of his friendly neighborhood banker suddenly becoming generous beyond anyone's wildest daydreams and bestowing on him the bank's entire resources, the dreamer need not hope the fantasy will come true. Dream probabilities may well be realized in life, but impossibilities remain impossibilities . . . wishful thinking notwithstanding.

Barber—The cutting of hair is symbolic of the castration idea. After Samson's hair was cut (courtesy of Delilah), he became weak and helpless; his potency was drastically reduced. A barber, as a man who cuts hair, appears symbolically in the dream world as a figure of strength who reduces other people's strength—specifically, their sexual potency, or manliness. If a woman dreams of herself as a barber she is casting herself as Delilah; probably she seeks to dominate men, or she is envious of their maleness. If a man dreams of himself as barber, in all likelihood he wishes he could reduce the potency of other men or of a particular man. When he dreams of himself as being shorn, it usually means that he is afraid of having his own potency reduced either by the person who appears in the guise of the barber or by some circumstance. Should a woman appear as his barber, he is probably indicating his own fear of being dominated by women or a lack of confidence in his own potency. In some cases the castration fear is accompanied by or replaced by an even more deeply hidden castration wish of the male to further his female qualities. (This should not be taken to mean that such a dreamer necessarily has any homosexual leanings, for every human being has both masculine and feminine qualities.)

If a woman should dream of being in the presence of a barber, she may be revealing fear and hostility toward men, which in turn may be a cover-up for her own desires. Finding her own sexual feelings unacceptable and possibly frightening, she dreams up a barber to protect her from men by reducing their strength and the source of her temptation. Of course, it is entirely possible that the woman who dreams of a barber may simply be reliving a horrendous visit to the barbershop with her three small children, or a young man may be resenting the haircut imposed upon him by his father, but even in these cases it is often true that the daytime residue provides the symbolism of the night for the dreamer to use in telling his own story.

Bartender—We're back in babyland again, because the bartender is the individual who wields the bottle that satisfies man's infantile oral needs. . . . The bartender may thus represent a parental figure supplying the dreamer with mother's milk, or something more or less like it. One who dreams of a bartender may be missing Mother, or the sensual comforts and irresponsibility of childhood. On the other hand, a bartender is an individual who is paid to be convivial and serve up drinks, and may therefore represent a person whose friendship is of doubtful value. If the dreamer conceives of himself

37

as bartender he may either be revealing doubts about himself as a true friend or about his acquaintances, who may, he suspects, like him not so much for what he is as for what they can get out of him. If someone else plays the part of the bartender, the dreamer may be expressing his distrust of a friend or group of friends whose friendship is offered only at a price. Of course, if the bartender is only a small part of a general bar party scene, his significance must be weighed in the light of other characters and actions.

Bigamist—The person who dreams of himself as bigamist may be revealing his secret wish to have more than one love at a time, or he may be indulging in guilt feelings about desiring someone other than his mate. Then again, the bigamy dream could be expressive of the dreamer's deep love for his mate and his appreciation of her several good qualities. Perhaps he wishes that there were four of her, so he could love much more of her. . . . As for the unmarried dream bigamist, he is probably expressing an ambivalent attitude either toward marriage, himself as husband, or his love object(s). The person who dreams of someone else as bigamist is likely to be revealing his fear of being two-timed or otherwise cheated. At the same time he is expressing his feeling of inadequacy, for if he had full confidence in himself he would be unlikely to worry about not getting his fair share of devotion. Possibly his fear is that his mate is looking, or has a right to look, for another partner because our dreamer cannot adequately satisfy her sexual needs. For what it's worth, the old-time dream books (with one or two hair-raising exceptions) tell us that a bigamy dream is a contrary dream and usually denotes a happy domestic affair. Contraries, by the way, are not unknown in serious dream interpretation.

Body, Living Parts of—The human body is much too complex for complete dissection in these pages; and its parts, when dreamed of, have a significance so distinctive to the individual that any detailed attempt to discuss them in terms of probable symbolic values would be futile. But a glance at a few highlights may prove to be of interest as a guide.

Belly—The belly or abdomen may be significant to some in terms of womb or uterus, to others in terms of stomach, bladder, or "bellyache." Thus, depending on the dreamer and the associative circumstances, a dream of the belly may indicate a hope or fear of pregnancy, uneasiness about health, or the dreamer's sense that he has been "bellyaching" about something. If the dreamer is a woman and the one with a belly is a man, the woman may be reminding herself of the way to a man's heart or else she might be mulling over her resentment about his gluttonous habits.

Cheeks—This is the colloquial term for buttocks, and if you dream of a person's cheeks you are likely to be perpetrating a displacement from below upwards. Presumably you are too shy, even in your dreams, to ogle undraped buttocks, so you stare instead at facial cheeks. In doing so you are probably—in spite of your little stratagem—revealing sexual desire for the owner of the cheeks.

Ears—If one's ear is cut off that is one thing, and not a very nice thing, but to dream of cupping the ear to listen when one is being spoken to may indicate awareness that the dream speaker is saying something important. The speaker may either be a respected friend or the commonsense other-self of the dreamer. Or even his conscience. If the dreamer directs himself vainly to other people's ears, it may mean that he himself has been inattentive to the whisperings of his conscience.

Eyes—To some analysts, and some dreamers, the eye

has a phallic significance. Samson, it will be recalled, had his eyes put out after his hair was cut, and was thus additionally weakened. Oedipus blinded himself, in symbolic punishment, after discovering that he had committed incest. Thus, dream blindness may, to some, signify an unconscious fear/wish for loss of sexual power. To others, blindness in a dream may be the dreamer's message to himself that he has refused to face up to reality, or that he is groping in the darkness of ignorance or confusion. To people of spiritual inclination, a watching eye may be suggestive of the deity; and a person of clear vision, in a dream, is one conceived of by the dreamer as being possessed of insight and clarity of spiritual understanding.

Hands—A cold hand on the heart may represent the fear of death. A dream of "having one's hands full" may mean exactly that in the dreamer's waking life, as may a dream of "getting one's fingers burned." If a dreamer sees a dream character with beautiful hands, it is likely that he regards that individual as one who does good things or is generous and kindly. A dream of dirty hands suggests the dreamer's feelings about dirty work being done; if the hands belong to someone else, the dreamer is indicating his resentment or disapproval, and if the hands are his own the dreamer may be revealing his sense of guilt for something he is doing or has done. Blood on the hands may be similarly, if more strongly, interpreted.

Hair—As noted, a phallic symbol, although in many dreams it may have a purely individual significance or scarcely any significance at all.

Legs—Another phallic symbol, as one might suspect, but naturally not in every dream. An injured or amputated leg, as seen in the dream, suggests castration fear, although it is possible that the dreamer may feel he is a mental or emotional cripple. Or the crippling of the dream may be a form of self-punishment. There will be more about the serious side of injured limbs in a later chapter, but at this stage let us quote from the *Prince Ali Lucky Five Star Dream Book* in case he covers some areas neglected by modern analysts.

He says: "To dream of the symmetrical extremities of a woman denotes that you will lose your dignity and act very silly over some insipid creature. To dream that you have a wounded leg, implies a disappointment, possibly a loss. To dream that you have more than two legs, denotes that you have more irons in the fire than you can manage successfully. To dream that you can't use your legs, relates to poverty."

Poverty of the soul, perhaps? In spite of that crack about some insipid creature, maybe Prince Ali isn't too far wrong.

Mouth—If you dream of yourself as having a big mouth, you are admitting to yourself that you talk too much and possibly out of turn. If some other dream character has the big mouth, then you know what you think of him.

In a somewhat unpleasant, almost nightmarish dream situation, the dreamer may find himself pulling endless quantities of sticky or otherwise nauseating stuff out of his mouth. This could represent the dreamer's awareness of a sticky or difficult situation, or it may have reference to a venomous verbal outburst of which he is unconsciously ashamed.

A dream of a sore mouth may have sexual significance, since the mouth is a sexually sensitive zone. Thus the sore mouth may be the dreamer's protection against sexual activity. It is also possible that a sore-mouth dream may be pointing to a daytime visit to doctor or dentist.

Skin—Sloughing off of the skin may indicate awareness of a need for change, for removal of the outer covering and baring of the reality that lies beneath. Dreams of sores or eruptions of the skin suggest that the dreamer has a sense of something wrong within him, some nastiness that is bubbling to the surface. He may be in line for a physical checkup or a waking look into his conscience.

Teeth—See Teeth, Falling Out.

Further comments about parts of the living body are included under Injury, and the like.

Boss—Often, when the dreamer dreams of his boss, he is actually dreaming of a parent or other close relative who figured strongly in the childhood environment. When he endows his employer with attributes of people who were important to him in his youth, he is revealing that he regards his work-superior as a parental figure and indicating that he is, or would like to be, still a child.

In the case of other dreamers the transference is not nearly so strong but it is not dissimilar. If the dreamer dreams of his real boss, or someone he dream-thinks is his boss, he is likely to be revealing one of the following: He needs or wants a figure of authority to help him run his life and take over responsibility. He is resentful of not being fully independent and having to accept supervision. He is in awe of his boss or actually afraid of him. He feels that he is being bossed around, either by his employer or someone else.

When the dreamer casts himself as employer, whether he is or not, he is probably revealing either that he feels independent and masterful or that he wishes he were.

Bride (Bridegroom)—Brides are found more frequently in dreams than grooms, and they are usually found in the dreams of women. This is possibly the case because men don't usually think of women in terms of "brides," nor is the step into a new and more responsible life usually so great for a man as for a woman. If the dreamer herself is the bride, the chances are that she is expressing either: Her wish to leave the restrictions of her childhood home and create a new, independent life of her own. Her wish to find love and to marry. Her ambivalent feelings about getting married (particularly true if there is some dream hitch). Her wish to remarry —to start afresh, and do better next time. Her wish to recreate the happiness of her early married life. If the dreamer casts someone else as bride, it may be that she's simply jealous or she might be reminding herself to go out and buy a wedding present.

Bridesmaid—If a girl should dream of a bridesmaid she is either looking at herself as she is afraid she might always be; she actually is going to be bridesmaid at a wedding; or she is getting married herself and feels a little bit smug. When a girl dreams that she herself is the bridesmaid or minor member of the wedding group, she is probably revealing one or more of three thoughts: Fear that she is sexually inept or unattractive. Fear that she will never marry. Ambivalent wish to leave home and be independent and yet continue to enjoy the security of the family life she has grown up with.

Burglar—A burglar is, of course, someone who steals. Generally he takes something of value to someone . . . possibly jewels, or a woman's virtue. If the burglar is unidentifiable in the dream, the dreamer had best get to work to find out just who he is and what he stands for, or else concentrate his attention on the object of the theft. If the burglar is the dreamer himself, the dreamer may be revealing a feeling of guilt that he has stolen, or wants to steal, certain objects or qualities—possibly a

43

woman—from someone else. Or he may *wish* to steal power, financial status, possibly potency, from another man. It should be remembered, though, that a crime is a crime, and even a burglar—a criminal—may commit a crime other than burglary. One crime, in a dream, may substitute for another. Perhaps the dreamer has in mind not a theft but something else that he has done wrong. Committed some sort of forbidden action? The dreamer must sort that out by himself.

Freud said that dreams of burglars have their origins in infantile memory, from those days when we woke up in the middle of the night and saw somebody standing there. In our sleepy state we were barely aware that the dim figure was father. We thought it was a burglar and we were anxious, and now we have anxiety dreams of a burglar while all the while thinking of Dad.

Butcher—A butcher is, probably unfairly, frequently associated with strength, violence, bloodletting, and chopping up. If one should dream of the corner butcher it is unlikely that the dreamer has any personal feeling for the man, but he does have a personal feeling about someone else to whom he attributes some of the butcher's characteristics. For example, an individual may dream-characterize his surgeon, or his wife's surgeon, as a butcher; or a woman may be dreaming of a sexually violent lover in the guise of butcher.

One who dreams of himself as butcher is probably revealing a closely guarded desire to hack at, skewer, and carve up someone else, or at any rate to lash out at something and release the pent-up hostility and violence within him. One who dreams of someone else as a butcher indicates his fear of that person. A woman who dreams of a butcher may be expressing fear and revulsion at the idea of the shedding of blood (her own) and the penetration of flesh (also her own) by a knifelike object. Since there are such people as woman butchers, the woman dreamer may also be expressing hostility and aggression and the need to hurt.

Cannibal—To dream of a cannibalistic meal is to dream of something that ought not to be done, that ought not to be touched—possibly a forbidden love object. Usually such dreams are accompanied by feelings of anxiety, very likely based on a fear of being found out in the forbidden activity. In some cases, that which is being devoured represents not so much a love object as the object of the dreamer's sadistic hatred. An occasional dream of a cannibal feast may mean no more than that the dreamer would like to gobble up his loved one, or that he is afraid of being emotionally devoured by someone else. When the dream is accompanied less by anxiety and revulsion than a faint sense of guilt, it may indicate the dreamer's awareness that he is "living off" somebody, possibly his working wife or his generous father.

Child, Children—Many parents do not have to look very far to find interpretation for their dreams of children. There is always some distortion, but a look at the total dream picture and its emotional coloring usually provides the explanation. Still, dreams of children often mean far more than readily meets the eye. (See Baby.) Some analysts hold that the dream child symbolizes the Christ idea. In fact, many dreamers have reported "seeing" a beautiful child wearing a strange looking hat, or halo. Dreams of nursing a child may indicate the nourishing of high ideals; dreams of killing a child may indicate the loss or destruction of high ideals. A dream of seeing, or being, a little child crawling may be suggestive of self-awakening and a groping toward spiritual truth. Prince Ali takes a somewhat different tack: "To dream of children is a splendid augury. If a woman dreams of giving birth to a child, it denotes a legacy or other good fortune. If she be a maid and dreaming the above, she should exercise much care or she will lose her virtue."

Convict—The convict, or prisoner, is usually someone who has been confined to a prison after having done something wrong, although of course there are cases of unjust imprisonment or other confinement. One who dreams of being a prisoner, or changing places with a convict in jail, may be admitting to himself that there is some strong, antimoral impulse within him that must be held in check; or that he has done something reprehensible (certainly guilt-inducing) that makes him deserve confinement. In some cases the dream may be a kind of warning or insight of some attitude or behavior pattern of the prisoner that may entrap him unless he changes his course. Perhaps he is thinking of an unwise marriage, or pursuing an unacceptable habit, and the dream is telling him to call the whole thing off before he gets hopelessly boxed in. In other cases the dream meaning may be much more direct: The dream convict or prisoner may feel trapped in a situation from which there seems to be no escape, or feel thwarted in his struggle to reach his goals; or he may wish that he could entrap and thus have custody of someone else.

Cook—A cook is the embodiment of one who provides nourishment, one of the essential forms of which is love. The dream cook, therefore, may be symbolic of the dreamer's mother, wife, or other loved one, or possibly of the dreamer herself. If the dream cook prepares tasty food and it is spurned, it indicates that the love gift is not wanted. If the cook prepares a delicious meal and then does not serve it, the implication often is that the dreamer has been offered or promised love that has not actually been given. If the dream cook serves up a delicious meal which is thoroughly enjoyed by the recipient, it may be possible to assume that the love gift is very satisfactory to the dreamer. Of course, if the dreamer *is* the cook, this may represent wishful thinking, but if the dreamer is the diner his dream does indicate that he is happy in his love. If the dreamer finds the food inedible it is a fair assumption that he is dissatisfied with the love gifts he is receiving. And if the identity of the cook is impossible to unveil, it may mean that the dreamer is yearning for love from someone, anyone, or anything.

Corpse—Dreams of corpses are seldom pleasant, but they are not always related to physical death. Sometimes they are about the death of love or hope, or the end—not necessarily unwanted—of a particular situation or relationship. However, it is often true that, if the dreamer casts another individual in the role of corpse, he probably has a deep wish for the removal, by death or otherwise, of that individual, or of some other individual disguised by the dream corpse. Or perhaps the dreamer is expressing the fear that he is losing his loved one. When the dreamer dreams of himself as corpse, his dream may be indicative of one or more of several dream thoughts: He may, genuinely, not be feeling well; he may be lying in bed "feeling like death." He may have a fear of death because of his awareness that he is no longer as young and strong as he used to be, or he knows that he has a serious ailment. He feels that he has done something wrong or had "bad" thoughts, and that he should be severely punished. He wishes for death as an escape from an intolerable problem situation. Or he is actually longing for the peace and quiet of death after a full and active life. The interpretation of the dream must, as usual, depend in large part upon the coloring emotion and the condition or demeanor of the corpse. (See also Dead Person and Dying/Death.)

Criminal—One who dreams of himself as a criminal is revealing his sense of guilt at breaking a law, violating his own moral code, or possibly hurting someone. One who dreams of another as criminal reveals his belief that someone else has committed a wrong.

Crowd—A crowd of people in a dream may be indicative of a secretive aspect of the dreamer's nature; the crowd is hiding him, or something about him. Or the crowd may be a camouflage for a particular person hidden within it, one about whom the dreamer does not wish to think or admit to thinking of. A crowd or group of people peering or staring at the dreamer may represent the dreamer's feeling about public opinion or perhaps the attitude that his friends might take if they only knew . . . whatever it is that is worrying the dreamer.

Dead Person—To dream of following or joining a person who is actually dead, even though he may appear in the dream as alive, suggests that the dreamer may be harboring the death wish or suffering from depression. When youngsters dream of joining, or being called by, someone who is dead, it is likely that they are weighted down by feelings of helplessness and misery. Life seems hopeless to them. (The feeling is usually temporary.)

When there is no action such as beckoning or joining, and the dead person simply appears as alive and normal in the dreamer's presence, then the indications are that the person is spiritually alive in the dreamer's mind and probably still loved and missed. However, there is a hint of the death wish in such a dream, for dreaming of the dead means that the dreamer has the idea of death

48

in mind. There is nothing remarkable or frightening about this; we all think and wonder about death, and in the lives of most of us there comes a time when the prospect of death is more appealing than alarming. Other dreams of the dead-returned-to-life, particularly if accompanied by feelings of fear or oppression, can only be interpreted in the light of the dreamer's own specific recollections and associations.

Dentist—To dream of going to the dentist may reveal the dreamer's deep-down knowledge that he is due for a dental checkup, but since to many of us the dentist is symbolic of pain and fear the dream-dentist is usually representative of an individual or situation that is fearsome, hurtful, or to some degree destructive. Thus the dentist may represent any feared person of the waking world, or he may represent something less tangible. A dentist pulls teeth; the person who dreams of a visit to the dentist may be expressing the fear of losing a vital part of himself, namely, his potency. Or he may be expressing the fear/wish for his own death. The dreamer who casts himself as dentist may be expressing his wish to hurt, his need to act out his feelings of hostility and aggression.

Detective—A detective in the dream is usually representative of the dreamer's conscience and may indicate that he has something to hide. The dreamer may fear being found out, or he may wish that he could unburden himself, or he may feel he deserves punishment for the hidden misdeed (which is almost as likely to be imaginary as real).

Doctor—To a patient, a doctor *is* a doctor, and the doctor in the dream is likely to be a caricature of the real person—the details of the caricature depending on what the patient thinks of his doctor. Also, a doctor is a figure of authority, sometimes a father figure, often an almost godlike being with the power of life and death. A dream doctor is representative of an individual who is gentle, comforting, healing, powerful, and authoritative. One who dreams of a doctor is either dreaming of someone who is much loved and admired, or is wishful of finding such a person. In some cases the dreamer wishes not only for a source of comfort and strength but for relief from pain . . . not necessarily a pain that is consciously experienced.

Driver—A driver is an individual who is more or less in control of his vehicle and direction. The dream-driver is operating a vehicle which usually symbolizes either his life or his physical body, and the interpretation of the dream depends on how he operates the vehicle. In casting himself as driver, the dreamer at least thinks of himself as being in some sort of control rather than being driven by someone or something else. The dreamer-driver shows himself to have some spirit of independence and some sense of self-mastery. It may not last long, but it's something nonetheless. What may put a curb to the surge of confidence and independence is a shattering encounter with the back of a truck, or a light pole that somehow gets in the way. Such carelessness indicates that the dreamer-driver is careless of his drives; that is, that he has lost or is losing control over certain basic cravings that are better kept in check. Unless he swiftly takes more competent charge of his vehicle he is in danger of being overwhelmed by an undesirable and uncontrollable impulse. On the other hand, if in the dream he does see traffic danger looming and manages to avert disaster by quick thinking and skillful driving, the indication is that he has brought the undesirable impulse under control. If the dreamer-driver has no difficulties with the mechanism of his car, with his speed, with his direction, with other traffic, or with the police, the indications are that he has his life in pretty good control.

It is also possible that the dreamer is expressing a wish to be independent, and to arrive at his chosen destination in his own way under his own steam. And if the dreamer casts another dream character as driver, the indications are that the dreamer feels he has little control over his own destiny.

Drunkard—One who dreams of being a drunkard may be admitting to himself that he has been a little heavy on the bottle lately; in his innermost thoughts he may be realizing that he is heading for trouble unless he moderates his drinking. Or he may wish to be the bottle-baby he once was, long ago, totally without responsibility and the need for self-control; all he wants is the sensual satisfaction of the bottle and being babied. If a dreamer should cast another character in the role of drunkard, the chances are that there is a real drunkard or incipient drunk in the dreamer's life who is causing unhappiness, or that someone else close to the dreamer is acting like a selfish, irresponsible child. Or else the "other" drunkard is the dreamer himself . . . trying to shift the blame for his over-indulgence or over-dependence onto someone else.

Dwarf—One who dreams of himself as a dwarf or midget is probably indicating his feeling of being outclassed, overpowered, and undercut by others or by circumstance; or revealing his awareness that he is emotionally stunted. Even if the dreamer dreams of

51

someone else as dwarf he is revealing his own sense of inadequacy, for such a dream suggests that he wishes to cut someone else—a specific someone, or a symbolic anyone—down to manageable size, and thus feel less helpless and ineffectual himself.

Enemy—The enemy who appears in the dream is almost always part of the dreamer himself, either a personification of his neurosis (which he knows is no friend to him) or an aspect of his personality which he unconsciously acknowledges as being alien or objectionable in some way. It is possible, too, that the dreamer may really have an enemy, or that he is battling in real life against what appears to be an inimical force.

Eve—Earth Mother, that's Eve, Mother to us all. Dream-Eve is thus likely to represent the dreamer's own mother, although to some dreamers the idea of a new beginning or of paradise may be of more significance. It is possible, too, that the dreamer knows someone named Eve, in which case he is either enjoying an explicit, nonsymbolic dream or else revealing that he associates his friend Eve with his mother or with paradise or a new beginning. It is also quite possible that a once-in-a-while dream of an "Eve" may have reference to a date or occasion, such as Christmas Eve or New Year's Eve.

Executioner—In most dreams employing the execution device, the dreamer himself is both executioner and victim. When the dreamer experiences his own dream-death by execution, he is revealing his attempt to get rid of that part of himself that he considers to be "wrong" or alien or destructive; he is attempting to destroy the enemy within. In some dreams, when the dreamer is the

52

executioner and the victim is identifiable as someone else, it is probable that the dreamer is revealing his desire to cut somebody or something out of his life; in other such dreams the dreamer may be expressing deep hostility feelings.

Father—Dreams of one's father are often just that—dreams of one's father. What is important in interpretation is the interaction between the dreamer and dream-father, and what dream actions and characteristics the dreamer assigns to the father. The father in a dream may also represent something larger than life; he may be a figure of authority, the one above—even the Supreme Being, or God. It is possible, therefore, that the dreamer is expressing a wish to submit to higher authority, spiritual or otherwise, or that he is revealing his resentment or even fear of an authority figure.

Fireman—Fire is a dream symbol of lust and excitement, of love and sexual passion, of anger and destructiveness—of passion. The dream fireman is a figure with the authority and ability to control the blazings of these various passions. Thus, one who dreams of a fireman is expressing his wish to quench the emotional fire within, or revealing his need for help in putting down the blaze.

Foreigner—Context and specific action is important as usual, but when a dream of a foreigner or foreigners is accompanied by fear the dreamer is likely to be expressing a dual concept: an awareness of his own racial prejudice (which in itself is a kind of fear), and a fear of what is foreign within himself . . . an alien something that he does not understand or recognize or wish to face.

Gardener—A garden is a plot of ground where plants, flowers, fruits, vegetables, or herbs are cultivated; it is something that is beautiful, productive, well-planned, and usually gratifying to the gardener-owner. One who dreams of being a gardener is likely to be expressing his own well-planned, controlled attitude toward the attainment of something gratifying and beautiful—frequently, his erotic goals. Or he may be expressing his deep satisfaction with some well-handled, productive work that he is doing. One who dreams about another as gardener is likely to be suggesting his—probably *her* —desire for the planting and growth of a living thing . . . a child.

Hairdresser—One who dreams of the ministrations of a hairdresser may be revealing a need to prepare for something, to get organized, to be ready to face a situation. Or she may be revealing a wish to be more attractive sexually.

Jailer—The jailer of a dream is (usually) keeping an impulse or desire in check, an impulse or desire considered by the dreamer to be improper or immoral. Therefore the dreamer is actually dreaming about his own conflicting attitudes: On the one hand he wishes to indulge in certain desires, and on the other he has set up a guard against these "criminal" impulses. His dream story may be expressing his need for such a guard or his resentment against such a guard, self-imposed though it may be. Or, on a less symbolic level, the dreamer may be expressing resentment against an individual who has trapped him into a jail-like situation; or he may even be wishing that he himself were jailer in charge of a particular prisoner, and thus in a position to prevent that individual from ever leaving him.

Jekyll and Hyde—It is unlikely that many dreamers actually dream of Dr. Jekyll and Mr. Hyde, but a vast number of most dreamers' dreams employ the split personality device. This trick, discussed before in more general terms, permits the dreamer to express various aspects of his own personality in the shape of other dream characters. Police officer and criminal, for instance (typical Jekyll and Hyde opposites), may represent the conscience of the dreamer and his forbidden impulses. In some dreams the dreamer's several selves may be represented by several characters, some conflicting and some getting along in reasonable harmony. The nicer the character aspect, the more likely the dreamer to play that part of his character himself. The repressed, undesirable aspects of the dreamer's personality are likely to be displaced, or projected, into the other characters. Thus it is possible that in a dream involving several characters, *each* character represents a component of the dreamer's personality and any interaction or conflict between them is a projection of the dreamer's own inner conflict.

Judge—The dream judge symbolizes authority, justice, and the power to punish. To some dreamers he symbolizes God Himself, and in such cases he is likely to be seen as a venerable and awesome figure weighing the dreamer in the balance and pronouncing judgment. To other dreamers the dream-judge is a figure of somewhat less authority, namely a parent; and to most dreamers the dream-judge, of whatever degree of authority, represents the voice of conscience. One who dreams of himself as being tried before a judge is either looking deep within himself for justification and approval for something he has done, or he is expressing a feeling of guilt and perhaps a wish for punishment for a misdeed that he may or may not have committed.

Jury—The function of a dream-jury is similar to that of a dream-judge, but to the dreamer the jury probably has less authority and more down-to-earth significance. A jury presumably consists of one's peers, and a dream jury is likely to signify public opinion. The dreamer might have a secret fear of what society would think of him if his secret impulses—or possibly a course of action—were to become public knowledge.

King—A king is a majestic, larger-than-life figure who, in dreams, always symbolizes authority. In most dreams he represents the dreamer's father; in some, he represents the Heavenly Father.

Knight—In these unchivalrous times it is seldom that one dreams of knights, but we are still occasionally reminded of them by television commercials or lavish film productions. Unreal as they are in our daily lives, so are they in our dreams; they represent an unreal idea of romance and bravery. Still, they *do* represent that idea, and one who dreams of being swept off her feet by a knight is indulging in the wishful thinking of the incurable romantic, or the immature. One who dreams of being a knight is probably quite young and likely to dream of other dashing figures on other nights—although to a few dreamers the emphasis may be upon the armor, a practically impenetrable covering that isolates the dream-knight or makes him seem unreachable.

Officer, Military—A military officer is a figure of authority, one who not only gives orders but who has the power to enforce them and to punish those who disobey. He has command over people; he has control over them. To dream of being under the command of a military officer suggests that one may feel resentful of someone who is running his life for him, or that he may wish for a commanding figure to guide him and tell him what to do. If the dreamer sees himself as a military officer, he is either expressing his wish to be commanding, authoritative, respected and powerful; or he is revealing his vision of himself as a pretty important fellow. If the dream figure is somewhat inflated, so much more revealing the vision.

Passenger—When a dreamer casts himself in the role of passenger in a vehicle, the chances are that he is revealing himself as a passive individual who feels, and actually is, dependent upon others. He may even feel that his destiny and way of life are completely in the hands of someone else. A passenger in a taxicab is in a somewhat different position, because he does give the orders and has decreed the destination; this kind of dreamer-passenger can be said to feel in control of himself and his destiny *unless* the dream-driver disobeys, loses the way, or somehow comes to grief. If something of this sort occurs, it may mean that the dreamer-passenger is telling himself that he has misplaced his trust. But ordinarily the dreamer-passenger is the kind of person who takes the back seat in waking life and probably doesn't even have the energy to be a back seat driver.

People—This vague and faceless category includes those vague and faceless characters who hover on the fringes like extras with nothing whatever to do. They serve a purpose, though; they are the onlookers, who represent public opinion or a kind of Greek chorus of conscience. They might be the people in the hall, listening; or the people in the bedroom, looking on; or the people in the street, gazing at your naked form; but they are *there,* wispy embodiments of the dreamer's thoughts. The dreamer is able to transfer whatever shock or embarrassment he may be feeling to the faceless watchers, or he may use them and their disinterested reaction to prove that strolling naked down Fifth Avenue isn't really very unusual at all.

Sometimes in a dream a group of people or an unidentifiable individual will rebuke the dreamer or protest to him about something. Such people are nearly always representative of the dreamer's own conscience. Even if their attitude seems to be unduly harsh they are *still* creations of the dreamer's own mind, and their parts have been written for them by him.

Then again, sometimes in a dream one or more persons will appear who don't seem to be doing very much of anything. Possibly they are identifiable as friends or relatives but they are not particularly advancing the plot. Unless they start acting up their reason for being there is simply that the dreamer has thought of them; they are personifications of the abstract ideas of Father, Mother, Lover, Friend, and so on. They "came into his mind."

Police—A dream policeman may represent authority, protection, punishment, conscience . . . or all four. One who dreams of the police or an individual policeman may be revealing guilt feelings for some breach of his own moral code and admitting to himself that he deserves punishment. (The misdeed may be actual, or it may be no more than a "wicked thought." The fact that the dreamer thinks he deserves punishment is not an indication that he really does. The more hardened the sinner, the less likely he is to harbor dream feelings of guilt.) Sometimes the dream policeman appears in the role of protector rather than punisher. When this is the case, the chances are that the dreamer is calling upon his own conscience—his own protector—to keep him from breaking the law, or giving in to his own antimoral impulses. For a minority of dreamers, and not necessarily criminals only, a waking-life policeman represents something other than protector of the just and nemesis of the unjust, in which case his dream appearance means something quite different, and very individual, to the dreamer.

Prince (Princess)—One who dreams of being, or being with, a prince is likely to be indulging in wish-fulfillment, or is perhaps thinking of someone as a "prince of a fellow." A girl who dreams of a princess is either dreaming of herself as the lucky daughter of a couple of very special people, or dreaming of a sister whom she considers to be a fine person—or a spoiled one. Generally the prince (princess) figure is a son (daughter) symbol rather than a symbol of royalty or glamor or wealth.

Prisoner—See Convict.

Prosecutor—The dream-prosecutor is the one who points the accusing finger at the defendant; he is, in fact, the dream-defendant's other self. In a sense he may also represent public opinion, but one does not usually worry about public opinion if one's conscience is entirely clear. The defendant and the prosecutor thus make up a typical Jekyll and Hyde team, the defendant representing the improper impulse and the prosecutor representing the dreamer's moral sense.

Queen—As a queen is the most beloved and influential woman in her realm and among her family of subjects, so is a mother the most beloved and influential woman in her home and among her family. The dream queen, therefore, usually represents the dreamer's mother. For those who are accustomed to using the word "queen" in

59

its slang sense alone, the dream-queen may represent something entirely different that would have to be interpreted in the light of the dreamer's associations.

Religious Figure—This category includes such dream figures as minister, priest, rabbi, nun, monk, saints, biblical characters, and other spiritual leaders of the past and present. The appearance of such a figure in a dream suggests that the dreamer feels a need or desire to be a better person, to be more loving and giving, more sincere and forgiving. The figure is a kind of conscience symbol, but not so much the accusatory conscience as the other self—the inner better half.

Servant—One who dreams of himself as a servant is probably indicating his feeling that he acts like a servant or is treated like one; in all likelihood he feels inferior or servile. It is also possible that he may feel humble rather than servile, and that he wishes to serve a worthy cause. One who dreams of himself as being a master of servants is likely to be revealing a certain arrogance or a wish to exercise authority over people to whom he considers himself superior. Specific servant figures may lend themselves to more specific interpretation by the dreamer himself.

Shadow of the Self—People very seldom dream such details as shadows, and when a shadow figure appears it tends to be more like a "shade" or ghost than a silhouette cast by the sun. Such a shadow may be interpreted as being that part of ourselves that we would like to cast out, or reject; it may be a sickness, a moral defect, or an emotional flaw; and it is probably something that the dreamer finds ugly and loathsome to him, or at least unpleasant. Rather than being alarmed by such a dream or its probable interpretation, the dreamer (upon awakening) should take heart in the thought that the first step in excising—or exorcising—the "devil" within is to know he's there, and the next step is to want to get rid of him.

Another shadow sometimes dreamed of is the shadow of another self, in this case someone else's self . . . a ghostly figure, apparently dressed in flowing white mist. Referring to Freud, we find that such a figure relates to infantile memory and that the ghost is really the Mother who made nocturnal visits to the bedroom of the sleepy child to make sure that he was properly tucked in.

Stranger—The stranger may be interpreted, in some dreams, as a symbol of the unconscious itself, for there is nothing more strange than man's own unconscious mind. In other dreams the male stranger may represent the dreamer's father. And in yet other dreams, strangers represent whatever is uncertain or unknown or difficult to understand. Sometimes the dream stranger represents a part of the dreamer's personality which he would just as soon not have to acknowledge; and sometimes the stranger represents some aspect of somebody else's personality. Real strangers, though, are not encountered in the dream. People who seem strange are merely difficult, not impossible, to identify—though they are not necessarily identifiable as people. (That nasty little man with the mean and furtive look? Why, a part of yourself that you have never cared for.)

When comparative strangers (that is, people we know very slightly) assume important dream parts, they do so because they remind the dreamer of something or somebody, or because they have some peripheral association with a conflict in the dreamer's life, or because they symbolize some aspect of the dreamer's life or personality. The dreamer uses the stranger to express ideas for him; whatever raw material is presented by the real-life stranger is snatched upon by the dreamer to shape a thought into a person.

We often dream of semi-strangers, of people we knew many, many years ago and have not seen or thought of since graduation or their wedding or something of the sort. They, too, pop up for a reason, and the reason usually is that something we experienced during the day or somebody we met reminded us in some small way of that friend of long ago. The reminding experience was probably of some consequence, for otherwise the dreaming mind, not concerned with people and things outside the area of the dreamer's personal conflicts, would not have bothered to dredge up the forgotten person.

Teacher—A teacher in the dream may symbolize one of the following: the dreamer's father; an individual or situation that is testing the dreamer; a person to whom the dreamer can, or wishes he could, turn to for instruction and advice; an authority figure with judicial powers; the dreamer's own feeling that he deserves criticism and perhaps punishment; the dreamer's wish that he himself could be a teacher or other figure similarly endowed with intellect or punitive powers or other enviable asset. Interpretation depends very much on the dream plot and what the dreamer actually thinks of teachers.

Tramp—To dream of a tramp, it says in the old-time dream books, is a suggestion that you write to your loved one. It is not a bad suggestion, but it isn't much of an interpretation. More than likely, to dream of a tramp is to dream of a self or other person who is a "bum" in behavior. If the dreamer casts himself as tramp the chances are that he regards himself as a material or moral failure; in his dream he may be asking himself how he could have sunk so low. Or he may be feeling guilty over some course of action or his treatment of someone close to him; he feels like the bum that he may or may not be. To dream of someone else as a tramp is to think of them as being crummy, irresponsible, possibly dirty, certainly unfit for the society of nice people like the dreamer. In the occasional dream the "tramp" may be a play on words: tramp, tramp, tramp, the boys are marching. . . . (Not so farfetched as it at first may seem; after all, the hobo-tramp does a lot of walking himself.)

Undertaker—The dream undertaker symbolizes death. The appearance of an undertaker in a dream suggests that the dreamer harbors the death wish for himself or for someone else. If the wish is on the dreamer's own behalf, then it is apparent that the dreamer has guilt feelings and a need to be punished. Or he may have less a wish than a fear that retribution will catch up with him. The more unpleasant the total dream, the stronger the guilt and fear. (Let it be emphasized again that the guilt feelings may be entirely misplaced. Some people feel no guilt after committing murder; others feel like flagellating themselves after thinking a forbidden thought.)

Watcher—A dream-watcher who simply looks on at the dream action and does little more than express mild interest or disapproval may represent public opinion, conscience, or some part of the dreamer's mind that is able to view the dreamer with detachment. The kind of dream-watcher who peers through windows suggests that the dreamer is a would-be Peeping Tom, a mental snoop, an exhibitionist, or afraid that some closely guarded secret is going to be found out. But the dream-watcher who appears more often in dreams than any other kind is the dreamer who watches his own dreams instead of actually participating in them. The person who watches rather than participates is one who does so in waking life as well; the active person almost invariably takes a very active part in his own dreams. If a person is a frequent observer of his own dreams there is a very strong likelihood that he is a daytime spectator as well, content to watch while others do. He is dependent on other people for his pleasures, and he tends to be dependent on them for many other things as well.

Watchman—The watchman of the dream is again a kind of conscience figure, one that stands on guard against any wrong move by an improper desire or impulse. He watches to see that no immoral actions are performed and that no forbidden wish runs around the place unchecked.

Witch—It is seldom that men dream of witches, but when they do they are probably—regrettable though it may seem—dreaming of their wives. And if they are dreaming of the loved one, they are almost certainly discussing with themselves how mean she has become and how badly she has let herself go since they were married. If a woman dreams of a witch she may be admitting to herself that she is behaving like one or that it's time she took herself in hand, although it's equally likely that she's dreaming of another woman. Sometimes, a woman's witch dream may be indicative of the dreamer's fear of losing her looks . . . of getting old and ugly.

On which cheerful note, we turn our attention away from people and focus it on the places where they may be found.

FOUR

Places and Scenes

We still tend to think of a dream as containing many outlandish components, one of them being the setting, but the fact of it is that we very seldom dream of exotic places.

About one-third of our dreams take place indoors, in some sort of building that is not always readily identifiable. It may be the dreamer's own house, or it may be a school building, a hotel, or a hospital, or simply a structure with rooms and hallways and stairs. Sometimes the nature or purpose of the building is significant; for instance, "to go back to school" is to do something considerably different from "spending the night in a motel." Sometimes the nature or purpose of the building is totally subordinate to the fact that it has particular rooms and areas that may be significant; the attic represents a high level of some sort, possibly mental activity; the basement is "low down"; the stairs are there to be mounted; and the doors and windows are for entering. In these characteristics may lie their dream significance.

Outdoors, fairly common dream sites are city streets, beaches, lakesides, decks of ships, gardens, mountainsides, highways, bridges, and what might be called general scenics—outdoor locations that we know are outdoors but can only describe in the most general terms. Dreams of being in some sort of conveyance are quite frequent, automobiles being in the lead followed by trains and boats and planes. The manner of handling the vehicle is significant, as is the very fact of being in something that is moving; movement is suggestive of doing something, of making progress, of getting somewhere; any obstacle or flaw or difficulty in moving is suggestive of a lack of progress. (For example, the plane won't get off the ground, the car stalls, the truck rolls backwards, the canoe loses its paddles; the dreamer is indicating doubts about his forward movement.)

The setting of the dream thus has a symbolic significance that must also be discovered if the dream is to be understood. What the dreamer feels and does in that setting is usually of primary importance, but quite often the significance lies not so much in *what* he is doing there as the *fact* that he is there. If the place is gloomy, why should he have chosen such a place? Or is it warm and mellow, with a feeling of sunlit happiness about it? The dreamer may reveal a lot about himself by his choice of dream locales. If he regards the world as a pleasant place he may dream of pleasant, natural scenes; if he regards it as wild and turbulent and frightening he may see it as a jungle, or some other hostile environment racked by wars and natural cataclysms; if he thinks of it as unfriendly and cold, he may dream of it as bleak and icy.

So look around you. The scenery may be more important than you think. It may not look like much, but lurking in it there is meaning.

Airplane—The airplane of our dreams is nearly always seen as a setting rather than as an object—a moving setting in which the dreamer is either pilot or passenger.

66

The pilot of the plane, like the driver of a car or the captain of a ship, is the man in charge, while the passenger is the one who goes where destiny (or his life pattern) leads him. To a degree the driver/passenger relationship is the same as it is when other dream vehicles are involved, but not altogether the same because relatively few dreamers are actually capable in real life of flying planes and can hardly be expected to do so with any great expertise in a dream. Thus, if a man dreams of himself as pilot, fine—he is the captain of his fate, and possibly master of his soul; but if he dreams of himself as passenger he is not necessarily dependent on the winds of fortune or someone else's skills—he is simply a man who doesn't know how to fly a plane, who regards the pilot as an airborne cabdriver, and whose airplane symbolism relates to something other than pilot versus passenger.

Some dreamers employ the airplane as a symbol of sexuality, because the plane has a kind of power and vitality that dramatizes the sexual urge and because it soars and swoops as does the sexual urge itself. Other dreamers use the plane symbol to represent the flow of their lives: To one man a trip in an airplane may signify the soaring of his hopes and ambitions; to another it may represent a moving ahead; to a third it may mean a wish that he could rise above certain problems; to a fourth it may indicate a sense of mastery; to a fifth it may be an escape from reality; to a sixth it may represent, either fearfully or wishfully, the last journey of all. More than anything, it is a sense of going somewhere . . . and the kind of trip it is reveals what the dreamer is really telling himself. When there is no takeoff, there is no progress; the dreamer is earthbound, getting nowhere. If there seems to be no destination, or if there is a destination that is never reached, the indications are that the dreamer doesn't want to go where he feels his life is taking him or that he is doubtful about his own goals. Perhaps he has no goals; perhaps he thinks they are unreachable; perhaps he thinks his choice has been unwise. But if the flight is smooth and the airplane arrives safely at its destination, then the chances are that the dreamer feels secure in his choices and that his life is going well.

And what if the plane crashes? It could mean that the dreamer feels his hopes have all come crashing to the ground and that he thinks of himself as a failure—perhaps one who walks away to try again another day. Or that he has lost control over his impulses, and they have brought him low. Or that he senses that he has seriously damaged a relationship or hurt someone, and in doing so has hurt himself.

Alley—To most people, an alley is a narrow, unpleasant, backyards street that ends in back doors and shabby places and blank walls. An alley as a dream setting usually indicates that the dreamer is experiencing feelings of anxiety or revulsion. A dreamer who dreams of being chased through an alley is expressing deep anxiety, especially if he finds himself up against a dead end with his pursuer close behind him. Something is catching up with him and boxing him into a corner. If he runs blindly through the alley, unpursued but frantically searching for a way out, he is probably indicating a sense of indirection or futility in his general life pattern or in a specific conflict situation. To the dreamer who regards a real-life alley as a squalid, grimy place, the dream alley represents a sense of something sordid in the dreamer's life; he is going through the back alleys to reach his goals, or he is going in through the back door to get what he wants, or he is taking a devious, unpleasant route. Or he may even be telling himself that he has the morals of an alley cat. His own associations to the dream will enable him to make the correct interpretation.

Amusement Park—This is a sensual, sexy setting, largely because of the types of motion and activity (merry-go-round, roller coaster, target-shooting, and so on) involved, and it is also a fun setting. Therefore a dreamer who sets his dreams in an amusement park is suggesting that he is thinking of sex, that sex is lots of fun, and that he is prepared to or would like to throw his inhibitions to the winds and thoroughly enjoy his sexual life.

Attic—The dream attic often represents the dreamer's own conscious mind. It is the top story of his mental structure, and perhaps also the symbol of his highest ideals. The more airy and uncluttered the attic, the more serene the individual.

Automobile—In an automobile, as in an airplane, boat, train, or kiddy cart, the dreamer is in motion; he is going somewhere to do something. The movement may represent any kind of "doing something," from nourishing an ambition to achieving great things, from running away to breaking up a relationship and even to dying. The driver/passenger relationship and the nature of the trip are the main tip-offs to the meaning. (See Driver.) If the dreamer dreams of a car that refuses to start, he is probably thinking of his own inability to get moving. If the car refuses to go in the right direction or if it resists the dreamer's efforts to control it, the indications are that the dreamer is doubtful of his own ability to steer a successful course through life or a particular problem situation. When the dream-brakes fail, the indications are that the dreamer feels he has lost control over the sex impulse or has in some other way failed to properly exercise his will power. The automobile, like the airplane, represents power, vitality, potency, sexual energy; and the difficulties in controlling it quite often relate to the dreamer's inadequate handling of his sexual conflicts. A speeding automobile represents sexual vitality, and if the speed brings driver and passengers safely to their destination then the probabilities are that the dreamer has a healthy, well-controlled sex drive; but if the speed results in a traffic ticket the indications are that the dreamer is none too satisfied with his own sexual conduct and feels that he deserves punishment.

Additionally, the automobile may symbolize the physical body of the dreamer, and its working parts may have a relationship to parts of the body. Here again, if the brakes are weak it is really the will that is weak; if the car drifts forward even though the brakes are applied the suggestion is that the dreamer suspects himself of exercising insufficient restraint in some area, and if it rolls backward the chances are that the dreamer feels he has done some backsliding already. In some cases, a dream of an automobile in poor condition may be the dreamer's reminder to himself to have a medical checkup.

Bank—A bank is a somewhat more complex symbol than one might at first think. It may directly represent some aspect of the dreamer's financial affairs; or it may be considered as a depository of something of great value and beauty (spiritual treasures), or something dirty (filthy luchre), or something representing strength (the dreamer's own source of power and virility). Interpretation must depend on what the dreamer himself thinks of money; some people will equate it with love, some with filth, and some with power. Frequently, though, a deposit in the bank represents either storing up a treasure or storing up strength; and a withdrawal from the bank may mean either the loss of what is treasured or a loss of strength, that is, of virility or prestige. (See Money.)

Bar (Barroom)—A bar is, of course, a place where people drink, and its patrons can expect to find not only liquor but other patrons—in an atmosphere of conviviality and superficial friendliness. One who dreams of being in a bar may be revealing a need to satisfy his oral yearnings, that is, his desire for the comforting bottle of his babyhood; and he is probably, deep-down, an insecure, dissatisfied man. He may even be a very lonely one. If the emphasis of the dream is more on the conviviality than on the drink, the chances are good that the dreamer feels unloved and unhappy and is trying to seek his happiness in his dreams. On the other hand, if the emotional content and other details of the dream (plus the dreamer's own self-confessions) do not bear out the unloved-and-unhappy theme, it is possible that the dreamer is using the bar setting simply to let down his hair and lose his inhibitions. The bar is a sensual setting, and the dreamer may be thinking of satisfying his need for sensual stimulus—as a preliminary, probably, to satisfying his sexual appetite.

Basement (Cellar)—As the attic may represent the conscious mind, so may a basement represent the unconscious, that which is deep down within us. It may also be, as Dr. Emil Gutheil says, "the place where children may engage in forbidden games" . . . and not only children. Base unconscious impulses may be lurking in the dreamer, or thoughts of base things that he has done or may be tempted to do. One who dreams of a basement setting is very likely taking a look deep inside himself and not being too pleased with what he is seeing.

Bathroom—Dreaming of being in a bathroom suggests that the dreamer feels the need to cleanse himself in some way. It's entirely possible that he may be giving himself a subtle hint that he actually needs a bath, although it is more likely that the required cleansing is of a less physical nature. Perhaps the dreamer wishes that he could purge himself of something within that he feels is impure; or perhaps he has a sense of guilt over something said or done. In either case, he wants to wash it away. (See Water, Bathing.)

Battlefield—Since a battlefield is associated with aggression, so is a dream that is set on a battlefield or in the midst of battle. The dreamer is probably expressing strong feelings of hostility and aggression, or he is in a state of mental turmoil in which two or more antagonistic sets of ideas and impulses are massed against each other.

Beach—A beach is a sensual setting (sun and sand, water and waves, and possibly even a little lovemaking), and the dreamer who dreams of being at the beach is having a dream that is sexual in nature. He is revealing, too, that he has a happy and healthy attitude toward sex.

Bed (Bedroom)—A dream of a bed or bedroom may suggest thoughts about sex, illness, some sort of hidden or private activity, or the need for rest. The dreamer's associations and emotions must be brought to bear upon the bedroom scene before any interpretation can be made.

Boat—The boat, as a vehicle, tells much the same story as the automobile or airplane, except for the added element of water. (See Water.) A well-steered boat is a well-run life, while one that drifts about aimlessly suggests a dreamer who may be unready for independence and who feels inadequate to steer his own course. The boat ride in itself suggests the voyage of life, and all the dream details from destination to weather to fellow passengers to route to shipwreck add color to what the dreamer is telling himself. Obviously, plain sailing in the dream is likely to be indicative of plain sailing in real life. Here we have corroboration from Old Aunt Dinah herself, who says: "To dream you are in a boat upon a river, lake, or pond of clear water is very good, and denotes joy, prosperity, and good success in affairs. For a man to dream that he is recreating himself in a boat without fear, he will have comfort and success in his affairs; but if the water be rough and tempestuous, it falleth out contrary."

Bridge—A bridge is an object representative of a transition from one place or one thing to another. Thus, crossing a bridge or being on a bridge represents a transition in the dreamer's life. It may be a crossing from youth to adulthood, from high school to college, from family life to newlywed life, or from a state of conflict to a state of solution; or it may be the dreamer's preview of the crossing from life to death. Now for some advice from Prince Ali: "To dream that you cross a bridge safely tells that you will overcome your obstacles and rapidly speed onward toward success. Should the bridge go down from under you, beware of false friends."

Cage—A cage of any size symbolizes some form of imprisonment or restraint. A dream set in a cage, or a dream that features a cage, suggests something about the dreamer that is, or should be, held in check. If the dreamer dreams that he himself is in the cage he is probably expressing his feelings of being entrapped by some situation, of being bogged down or held back in something that he is trying to do, of being boxed in by his own inhibitions, or of needing to be restrained from giving free rein to his impulses. Seeing animals in a cage suggests that the dreamer is aware of his own pent-up impulses or restrained antisocial urges. Seeing someone else in a cage suggests either wishful thinking or the dreamer's awareness of another person's predicament. If the dreamer tries to liberate that person, the indications are that he would like to help the individual find a way out of his difficulties or free him (possibly her) from his inhibitions.

A cage, and all similar receptacles, can also be regarded as a female sex symbol. Only the dreamer can tell when that particular symbolism applies.

Castle—The castle as a dream object or setting may be no more than a castle in the air, but it is more likely that the dreamer is thinking of it in terms of an elegant, spacious house (see also House), possibly inhabited by the king and queen who represent his parents. One who dreams of being in a castle is likely to be expressing a desire for a better life, with fewer restrictions and greater richness. The desired improvement may be partly material, but the chances are that the dreamer is wishing for enrichment of character and a broadening of scope rather than for a move to a better neighborhood; he wants to be a better person. In some cases a dream of a castle may indicate the dreamer's wish to return to the secure days of his childhood, the castle representing the "large" home he lived in as a child (or that looked large to him when he was little).

Cave—A cave, particularly if it is subterranean, may represent the deeper levels of the mind itself or a place where something not very pleasant is hidden (dark thoughts or impulses). More often, though, it can be regarded as a symbol of the womb. One who dreams of going into or being inside a cave may have his mind on making love, or producing a child, or the security of the womb; he may wish to create something out of the cave, or stay there himself. In the latter case he is revealing a buried desire to relinquish all responsibility and become totally dependent on something or someone else.

Cemetery—When a dream is set in a cemetery the dreamer is probably expressing one of the following thoughts: a wish for the death of self or someone else; the fear of death, probably the dreamer's own; the death of love, or the end of a once-important relationship. Tombstones, however, usually have little to do with the idea of death; in dreams, they have a phallic significance, although they are also likely to stand for memories. Putting dead flowers down on a grave, or giving dead flowers to someone, is a rather strong indication of a death wish for that person.

Church—Dreams set in a church or other house of worship usually indicate that the dreamer would like to raise his spiritual sights or that he feels he needs guidance and help in achieving the moral standards that he has set for himself or that he feels guilty about being less moral than he ought to be. To some dreamers the church may symbolize a sanctuary, and that sanctuary may in turn be a private or closed compartment in the dreamer's own mind—containing his innermost thoughts or his inner life.

Courtroom—To some dreamers, a dream of being in a courtroom is associated with the idea of imperfect justice, either because the dreamer is cynical about the legal process or because he has a deep-rooted belief in God as the One Judge and only true dispenser of perfect justice. But most dreamers will use the dream courtroom as the setting for "real" justice. A dream of being in a courtroom suggests the dreamer's feeling that either he or someone else should be judged and presumably sentenced for some reprehensible urge or action. Persistent dreams of this sort probably indicate strong guilt feelings on the part of the dreamer. Even if the dreamer plays the part of judge or prosecutor, the chances are that he is judging or prosecuting himself.

Desert—One who dreams more than occasionally of being surrounded by desert scenery is likely to be indicating his view of the world, or his immediate world, as being a barren and cheerless place. Possibly he has a feeling of emptiness, and of isolation from other people; he may have no one to love, or he may feel separated in some way from those he does love. Almost surely he feels lonely, incomplete, and somewhat helpless. Or perhaps it is not so much his environment that is barren, but himself; he feels barren of ideas or emotions or creative energy.

Dining Room—The dream dining room has to do with the consumption of food, not only for the body but for the mind. However, food for thought takes second place, and the dining room of the dream is primarily a place where people satisfy their oral (and infantile, so the analysts say) needs, namely, eating and drinking. Those oral needs were originally satisfied by Mother, who served up love along with meals, and thus the dining room represents the place where love is found. One who dreams of being in a dining room or other eating place is thinking in terms of love and security; he may already have what he needs and be happy for it, he may wish for it, or he may wish to offer it to somebody else.

Elevator (Escalator)—It's a tired old joke, but it is perfectly true that to the man who runs the elevator life is full of ups and downs. So it is for the rest of us, and when we dream of riding in an elevator or on an escalator we are nearly always dreaming of the progress of our lives. If the elevator is ascending, the dreamer is either expressing his desire to rise in the world or his feeling that he is doing well. If the elevator is going down, it may be that the dreamer feels he is losing altitude in the pursuit of his career or some other important aspect of his life. Or he may be feeling depressed; his spirits are down, even if his fortunes are not.

Farm—A farm is suggestive of productivity, of the good things that come up out of the earth through the cooperation of man and (Mother) Nature. Therefore, to some people a dream set on a farm might be representative of a wish for love, marriage, and reproduction. To other dreamers, the produce of the earth is the food provided by a loved one, and their dream-farm may signify a desire to be loved and cared for. To yet other dreamers, the dream-farm may represent exactly that— the place in the country about which so many city-dwellers dream. And to a farmer, a dream about a farm is almost certainly a dream about a farm and will have to be interpreted through scrutiny of the details.

Garden—The garden, in its ideal state, is something beautiful, abundant, well looked after, and pleasing to both gardener and whomever might stroll through it. In a dream, it may be symbolic of the spiritual state or mental health of the dreamer; if the garden is well tended and the plants are healthy, then the indication is that the dreamer has a sense of well-being and gratification, and if it is dying from drought or neglect then the implication is self-evident. To some analysts and some dreamers, a lavish and well-planned garden is representative of an approach to sexual gratification that is tidily planned, appropriately restrained, and abundantly successful.

Grocery Store—This is another dispenser of food. One who dreams of shopping in a grocery store may be admitting to himself that he needs love and that he may have to pay for it in some way, or he might be commenting to himself about the need for a change in his diet.

Gutter—Anyone who dreams of being in a gutter probably feels that he is in one. Either he has sunk low in his own estimation, or he is aware of having certain thoughts or urges that he feels are low and contemptible.

Hallway—A dream hallway is much like a dream bridge; physically, it is a transition from one place to another, and symbolically it is a change or transition from one life state to another. However, it is the nature of the hallway and what happens in it that gives the real clue to the meaning of the dream; if the dreamer is chased through it by some terrifying figure, then the indications are that the transition is made complex by conflict; and if the hallway is dark and narrow it may relate to the first major transition of our lives—the one called birth. One who dreams of rebirth is almost certainly revealing a wish to repeat the very early part of his life, which in turn suggests that he may be pessimistic about his future.

Hill (Mountain)—Hills and mountains are to be climbed, and in the dreamer's success or failure at reaching for the heights lies the clue to most dreams in which a hill is a prominent part of the scenery. If the hill looms as an obstacle that cannot be negotiated, it is virtually certain that the dreamer feels blocked by an inner or outer circumstance in waking life. It follows that if he succeeds in his upward climb, he is revealing a feeling that he is capable of surmounting obstacles. (See also Climbing.) If a person dreams that there is something on top of the hill itself that he would like to reach, he is indicating that there is something in his life that he considers so far above him that it is almost unattainable —a spiritual ideal, perhaps, or a love object, or a high position with a firm. (See also Falling.)

Hospital—A dream set in a hospital is very often a mental note to the dreamer to take steps toward mending some emotional or mental imperfection. It may also express the dreamer's fear of physical illness and, therefore, death, or his wish to be looked after. The latter is the least common interpretation, because most people do not enjoy hospital stays and tend to associate hospitals with pain and worry and death.

Hotel—The hotel as a dream setting may be expressive of the dreamer's feeling that he is in a transitory state, since to most of us the real-life hotel is a temporary stopping place. To some dreamers, a stay in a hotel might have slightly shady connotations; there may be feelings of guilt over an extra-marital relationship that has been or is being conducted in a hotel or under hotel-like conditions (he has been using her house like a hotel). If the dream emphasis is less on the hotel aspect and more on the rooms and hallways, then the hotel may represent the dreamer himself and the many compartments of his being. Wandering through a suite of rooms may represent the process of recalling, of probing around within oneself.

House—A house in a dream often represents the dreamer himself, either body or mind or both. The upper and lower stories often represent the conscious and the subconscious respectively (see Attic and Basement). The various rooms relate to the activities normally associated with those rooms: The living room has to do with ordinary daily activities or the kind of material "living" that the dreamer is achieving; the bedroom is representative of sleep, the need for rest, sexual activity, or something private; the kitchen, dining room and breakfast nook have to do with food and emotional nourishment; the study is associated with work or mental nourishment; the bathroom relates to cleansing and purging; and the playroom is for play. What happens in these rooms, and who it happens with, is usually the key to the dream, but anything unusual about the house itself is also of importance. A house in need of repair suggests a dreamer in need of repair, either physically, emotionally, or spiritually. A house that is in good condition, with many lovely, well-appointed rooms, suggests a dreamer who is healthy and serene; and a house that is particularly beautiful and spacious suggests a dreamer who is wishing for a roomier, less restricted and more meaningful life. The atmosphere of the house is also significant. A house that is airy, bright, cheerful, uncluttered, and reasonably well organized suggests a dreamer with those same characteristics, and one that is cheerless, dark, and disorganized suggests a dreamer who has a number of negative characteristics or qualities, with pessimism and a feeling of depression probably heading up the list. And a house that loses its roof because of some explosive force or high wind suggests a dreamer who is thinking of raising the roof or "flipping his lid."

Sometimes the house of the dream represents not so much the dreamer himself as his feelings toward the people who inhabit any house that has real-life significance to him, for instance, the house in which he presently lives or one in which he spent his formative years. Again, the atmosphere, state of repair of the house, and actions of the various dream characters must all be considered in interpretation.

Island—One who dreams of being on an island is likely to be revealing either that he feels isolated from others or that he would like to cut himself off from a real-life situation.

Kitchen—The kitchen, where food is prepared, represents the warm, central core of the house. A dream set in a kitchen indicates that the dreamer is probably content with the love and warmth that he gives and receives in life; or he may be wishing for more. If the kitchen itself is incomplete, or if the house of the dream lacks a kitchen, then the indications are that the dreamer feels himself or his way of life to be incomplete. He may feel he is emotionally starved, or incapable of giving freely of himself.

Laundry—When a dreamer chooses a laundry as a dream setting he is usually revealing awareness of his need to cleanse himself in some way, possibly literally but probably figuratively. He feels soiled; there are stains upon him that he would like to wash away.

Merry-Go-Round—As part of an amusement park scene the merry-go-round is indicative of sexual pleasure; the motion and the general atmosphere are suggestive of this. However, if the emphasis in the dream is on the circular movement of the merry-go-round, it is likely that the dreamer feels he is going around in circles instead of making forward progress in his life.

Museum—A museum is, in a literal sense, a storehouse of old memories. Thus a dream museum may symbolize the dreamer's mind, the storehouse of his memories. A dream set in a museum may be a retrospective dream in which the dreamer visits his mental storehouse to look again at the scenes and happenings of his past.

Party (Picnic)—Dreams of being at parties, picnics, beaches, dances, and the like are strongly indicative of a dreamer in a sensual, pleasure-seeking mood, with sex at the head of his list of pleasures.

Precipice—One who stands at the edge of a precipice is one who is on the brink . . . of something. A dreamer who sees himself standing near the edge is probably expressing doubts about himself. Is he about to make a terrible mistake . . . take a moral fall . . . plunge into catastrophe . . . or die?

Prison—Prison dreams are suggestive of enforced restraint, confinement, and punishment. One who dreams of being in a prison may be admitting to himself that something in his behavior pattern has made him a prisoner of himself: excessive drinking, over-eating, negative thinking, or other habit/addiction/self enslavement. Or the prison dream may mean that the dreamer has guilt feelings about real or imaginary misdeeds or urges and feels that he should be restrained and punished; that he is afraid of retribution for something he may or may not have done; that he feels confined and helpless in a life situation; or that he feels unable to free himself from his inhibitions. An escape from prison might indicate a triumph over the restrictive part of the self, or it might suggest a desire for improvement in the dreamer's worldly or inner life.

Quicksand—A dream of being sucked into a quicksand suggests the dreamer's fear that he is being bogged down by an inner or outer circumstance, and that without help he will go under completely; or it may indicate the dreamer's fear of death; or it may suggest the dreamer's feelings that he is being dragged into the mud by his own immoral activities or some force outside himself.

Restaurant—A place where love is served . . . and sensual appetites are sated. Interpretation depends on how satisfied the dreamer is with the service and the meal. (See Dining Room and Kitchen.)

River—A large and rolling river in a dream is suggestive of the thought of death. Emotional coloring, other details of the dream, and how the dreamer feels when he wakes up (depressed, sad, or serene) must be taken into account when probing into the meaning. In some cases the river might have a long way to go before it reaches the sea which is death, and thus may represent the flow of life rather than its ending. (See Water.)

Road—The road of the dream is the road of life, and a fork in the dream road suggests that the dreamer feels himself faced by a difficult choice. One who dreams of taking the wrong road is probably admitting to himself that his chosen way of life is morally wrong, and one who dreams of a roadblock is admitting to an awareness that inner obstacles stand between him and his life goals.

School—Some dreams of being back in school are simply recollections of things past, and some reflect a desire to return to a time of irresponsibility and dependence on others. The latter suggests a degree of immaturity on the part of the dreamer and his wish to dodge the necessity of making adult decisions and choices. Depending on the atmosphere and action of the dream, the dreamer may (quite maturely) be telling himself that he is immature and still has a lot to learn; that he has been acting in a childish way; or that he has unfinished business to attend to. For some dreamers the return-to-school dream may be an expression of regret for not having finished school or completing higher education.

The examination dream may be either a reflection of anxiety or a sort of self-reassurance. In such a dream the dreamer is usually in a state of turmoil and tension over the prospect of taking an examination for which he is totally unprepared—even though he has probably actually taken it and passed it in real life. Sometimes these dreams can be interpreted as meaning that the dreamer is ill-prepared for the challenges and tests of real life and possibly ill-equipped even in his chosen field, which in turn is an indication that he is dodging the important issues of his life and suspects that he will some day have to face them under trying circumstances. Again, the examination dream may be the dreamer's own way of accounting to the Final Examiner; his conscience scores the test and usually finds him wanting. Quite often, the dream examination is a test of the dreamer's self-confidence, and occurs when he is about to make an important decision about career, marriage, or something of equal importance; then the dream indicates that he is unsure of his ability to pass the particular life-test that he is facing. How is it possible to be reassured by a dream of this nature? Well, some analysts say that the examination dream may serve as a reminder of tests already passed, that the dreamer may be recalling not only the anxiety preceding the examination but the fact that it actually *was* passed, and that if he could pass one test that was difficult and anxiety-provoking he can pass another that at the moment seems practically insurmountable. Freud suggests that the dreamer can, upon awakening, put it to himself in this light: "Don't be afraid of tomorrow. Think of the fear you suffered before the examination and, in view of the fact that everything turned out well, see how senseless it was to be afraid." Of course, if the dreamer failed his real-life examination because he had not done his homework, the dream may be considered as a reminder to him that he cannot hope to succeed unless he works at solving his problems.

Stairway—A dream in which a stairway is an important locale is an erotic dream; the dreamer ascends and descends, twin actions which symbolize sexuality. The same is true of a climb up or down a ladder, although both stairways and ladders may also be considered the "ladder of success." The dreamer's own associations must provide the true interpretation.

Station—A dream set in a railroad station, bus station or air terminal suggests a dreamer in a transitional or waiting state. The journey to be undertaken is the journey of life, and the station is the point of embarkation or change. To some dreamers, a station setting indicates a wish to escape from something or a desire to head for a particular goal. The chances for fulfillment of the wish are indicated by the dreamer's success or failure in

85

catching his plane, bus, or train, and the ease or difficulty with which he procures his tickets and takes care of his luggage. If a number of problems present themselves, the indication is that the dreamer is ambivalent about the proposed "trip" or change. The nature of the difficulties helps to explain the meaning of the dream. A dream of another kind of station—a police station—usually has the same meaning as a dream of a prison.

Theater (Movies)—Dreams in which the dreamer finds himself in a theater may indicate that the dreamer wishes to escape from the problems of real life or that he would like to receive the adulation usually given to a star performer. If the onstage or onscreen performance is uppermost in the dreamer's attention, the chances are that he is watching a performance of some aspect of his own life—that is, what he is "watching" is a projection of his own problems and conflicts.

Train—The dream-train, like the airplane, automobile, and bus, is a forward-moving vehicle and symbolizes movement. Depending on the dreamer and his associations, the "movement" may be sexual energy or progress through life. In probably the majority of dreams that feature trains, the train is the vehicle taking the dreamer on the journey of life. The nature of the trip is usually the tip-off to the dream. If the dreamer sees the train passing him by, he may feel that life itself is passing him by. If he runs for and misses the train, he may be expressing frustration at lost opportunity or revealing a desire to relive an experience that he knows is not relivable. (For more about coming-too-late dreams, see Missing a Train.) In some cases the dream-train may symbolize the dreamer's desire to get ahead in life, or to escape from a difficult waking-life situation.

Tunnel—A dream set in a tunnel or other narrow sub-terranean passage may represent either the dreamer's wanderings through the deeper levels of his own mind or the dreamer's preoccupation with the idea of the womb and his fantasy-return to it. If the latter, the dreamer may be revealing his wish to return to the comfort and security (and, of course, irresponsibility) of the pre-birth state, or his resentment at still being trapped in a womb-like situation—overdependence on the mother or both parents, and an inability to free himself from the apron strings.

Water, Bodies of—A large body of water seen in a dream, particularly the great, wide-open ocean, quite often represents the dreamer's own unconscious mind. The vastness of the sea, the depth of it, and the mysteries hidden within it all combine to symbolize the vast mysterious depths of the unconscious. Thus a plunge into the depths may represent the dreamer's attempt to plumb the depths of his own mind, in which lie deeply repressed thoughts and old memories. If the sea is in turmoil it may mean that the dreamer is experiencing emotional conflicts in his waking life. Or, depending on the action that takes place in or on the water, a dream of the sea may be indicative of the dreamer's journey through life: The passage may be rough, or the dreamer may enjoy smooth sailing, or the craft may be aimlessly adrift.

Some analysts maintain that all water dreams are birth dreams, and probably most water dreams *do* relate in some way to birth, death, and rebirth. Circumscribed bodies of water such as ponds or lakes are often easily identifiable with the uterus, which in itself is the symbol of birth and life. Thus a dream with a body of water as the setting may represent the idea of creating or re-creating life. The dreamer may be expressing the wish to create life; or he may be revealing his desire to be re-born himself. In the latter case the suggestion is either that he wants to be a child again or that he feels the need for spiritual rebirth or rededication. The real-life symbol of being purified and born again in the baptismal rite; the dream symbol of the same thing is the dream-plunge into water. It is no contradiction that water is also a symbol of death; death is considered by many people as a rebirth into a new (probably spiritual) life. When a plunge into the ocean is interpretable as a dream-thought about death, the indications are that the dreamer neither wishes for nor fears death but regards it as inevitable—in fact, as a part of life itself. If the ocean is symbolic of birth, and if a sinking into it may be symbolic of death, then that reentry into the symbolic source of life is a return to life itself—a rebirth into death or into a different world.

As might be expected, water also has much sensual symbolism. (See Swimming.) If the ocean is the source of life, it is not surprising that tumultuous waves and tossing seas may be representative of surges of lustful feeling or the soaring of the sexual impulse.

Zoo—Dreams set in a zoo may indicate either that the dreamer feels himself hopelessly and humiliatingly en-snared by circumstances, or that he is disturbed by his own impulses and feels that they (or he) should be held in check, or caged.

FIVE

Creatures and Things

The complete dream contains more than people and scenery; it comes fully equipped with animals, plants, furnishings, and objects of various kinds. Any and all of these things may be symbolic of an idea in the dreamer's head; even an animal or object may actually represent some aspect of the dreamer himself. Taken in conjunction with other elements of the dream, therefore, any living thing or creature or inanimate object *may* cast considerable light on the dream. Only, it doesn't always. Sometimes a prop is just a prop, and that is reason enough for its presence. Often the clothes we wear in a dream are just things we have on and have no significance at all beyond the fact that we do have them on rather than off; a chair is just a thing we sit in and does not need interpretation unless it suddenly turns into an electric chair or starts rocking feverishly or is transformed into a horse; the dream-purse that the dreamer always carries to work with her in real life doesn't necessarily have any striking dream significance unless it is dream-stolen, lost, or ripped open to have some strange sharp object thrust into it.

Thus, many things vaguely seen in dreams or back-drops or sketchy details are merely there because they are the basic props of our everyday lives. It is when they *do* something in a dream, or play some ridiculous, nonsensical part, or feature in the forefront of the action, or are particularly noticeable in some way, that they reveal themselves as being of some importance. Often they reveal an attitude or conception of the dreamer, or possibly a fear, and as such may be extremely valuable in interpretation.

The dreamer's own associations are, as usual, of great importance in revealing the truth. Is the object or creature of the dream something he can associate with in real life? Has he seen any snakes lately? Does he use a gun in his profession? Is he afraid of dogs, fond of cats? Has the dreamer ever really broken any windows, stolen any money, encountered a crocodile or thrown a knife? Whether he has or hasn't must lend some color to the dream and give meaning to the dream object with which he is dealing or of which he is particularly aware. Dream decoders should bear in mind, also, that in dreams we manage to be very hypocritical—we tell ourselves small off-white lies, we try to pass the buck. For instance, it wasn't the burglar who broke the window but the dreamer himself, and the window wasn't really a window at all but a . . .

See Window.

Anchor—A dream featuring an anchor may suggest either that the dreamer feels secure and stable in his life situation, that he regards someone else as being his anchor or securing force, that he would like to be able to put down his anchor and become settled in life rather than aimlessly drifting around, or that he feels like a stick-in-the-mud who is weighted down by circumstance or himself.

Animals—Most of us regard even tame animals as wild to a degree; thus animals seen in dreams usually represent something that is wild, unbridled, or difficult to restrain within ourselves. Quite often animals—particularly horses and other semi-tame but vital creatures—appear as the embodiment of unbridled sexual vigor. Sometimes they are symbolizations of impulses, attitudes, and activities that the dreamer unconsciously believes to be characteristic of himself and of which he does not altogether approve. Laziness, hatred, hostility, rage, lust, vindictiveness, "bitching," "backbiting," and the like lend themselves readily to translation into animal form. The more vicious or destructive the emotion or attitude, the wilder and more aggressive the dream animal.

Unpleasant dream thoughts, too—those that the dreamer has tried hard to repress but that insist on surfacing anyway—may also appear in the guise of attacking animals or malevolent creatures. Enough of such thoughts adds up to a nightmare populated by weird beasts that threaten and claw and bite and cling. (See also animals listed individually.)

Ape—The ape—the creature that looks and walks like a man—appears in dreams as the symbolization of what is brutally strong, lustful, and uncontrollable in man. A dream of an ape is usually an expression of fear, either of the thought of sexual attack or of unrestrained lust on the part of the dreamer himself. Sometimes a dream of an ape suggests that the dreamer is casting a known individual in the role of a sexually vital (possibly crude as well as brutal) animal, or regards that person as inferior.

Apple—The funny thing is, the dream-apple usually symbolizes temptation, and to eat one is something like taking a bite of the fruit of the tree of carnal knowledge. And he who steals someone else's apples is stealing love that does not belong to him. . . . Though the dream-apple may represent temptation of any kind, the connotation is usually sexual. (A passing note: Old Aunt Dinah wisely says that sour apples signify contention and sedition, in which observation she is probably correct.)

Ass—The ass of real life is generally regarded as stupid and stubborn, and one who dreams of seeing an ass is likely to be admitting to himself that he has been acting like one.

Balloon—Balloons are usually symbols of the female breasts.

Banana—The banana of the dream is usually a phallic symbol. So is anything else of that approximate shape—carrots, cucumbers, and other roots, fruits, vegetables, and gourds.

Bat—Prince Ali says that "it is a bad omen to dream of those nocturnal creatures, it foretells troubles, afflictions, even death is included." The conclusion of other analysts is similar, though they feel that bats do not so much "foretell" future troubles as symbolize very present ones. Unacceptable thoughts appear in the guise of dream bats, swarming over the dreamer and getting in his hair or filling the dark and eerie caverns of his mind; pangs of conscience, too, quite often assume the shape of bats, and descend upon the dreamer in the darkness of night, when he has relatively few distractions to keep him from mulling over his misdeeds. Bats seen swarming around in a high place or tower are suggestive of bats in the belfry; the dreamer suspects himself or someone else of being not quite right upstairs.

Bird—Here we have another male sex symbol—the bird soars and swoops, and thrusts and pecks. On a somewhat more romantic level, the bird may also symbolize the abstract idea of love.

Bomb—The bomb of real life is explosive and destructive; so, usually, is the bomb of the dream. When a bomb appears in a dream, and particularly when it explodes, the dreamer is likely to be admitting that he has one or more urges or emotions that he cannot control; possibly he has an explosive temper, which hurts himself and those around him, or he has a sexual urge that he feels is becoming uncontrollable. An exploding bomb may thus symbolize either the eruption of rage or the explosive climax of the sex act.

Bull—Male sex symbol; one of those unbridled, vital animals referred to above. Or, to other dreamers, bulls may symbolize other dangerous impulses or "sinful" thoughts.

Carpet—A carpet seen in a dream suggests that the dreamer is admitting to himself that he has something to cover up, or he is expressing the idea of stepping or being stepped on. (As usual, individual associations to the idea of "carpets" are bound to bring up other meanings.)

Cat—Cat lovers will be less than delighted to be told that dream cats seldom bode any good, but that's the story according to the analysts. Cats are among the night creatures that symbolize unpleasant thoughts, and when we realize that as nightmare thoughts they keep the company of trolls and imps and ghosts and bats we can see at once that they are up to no good. Uncontrollable, spilled-over thoughts are very seldom pleasant;

93

neither are dreams of cats. (Yes, there are exceptions.) Cats are often representative of the uncanny and the strange, of some depth of the unconscious that is difficult and perhaps undesirable to understand, of some aspect of the personality that is mysterious and revolting and quite possibly evil.

In other dreams the cat symbol may represent a woman—possibly her beauty and sensuality, but more likely her trickiness and cunning and her spiteful cattiness. When no particular woman or evil thought is in mind, the dream cat serves as a female sex symbol; that is, as any woman, or the female genitalia.

Cherry—Yes. Female sex symbol. *Virginal* female sex symbol. The significance of the giving, taking, and stealing of cherries will be obvious. Other aspects of the dream are helpful in deciding whether there is hope or fear involved.

Clock—The clock or any other time-keeping device (watch, hourglass, sun dial, calendar) always carries the idea of time in the dream as in waking life. One who dreams of a clock is likely to be expressing one or more of the following thoughts: that time is running out (in which case the hands of the clock *may* be racing) on life or a particular project; that an opportunity has been or is about to be missed; that there is much left to do and little time to do it in. When a clock is seen in a dream the idea of death is nearly always hovering on the sidelines—time keeps passing, lengthening the past and shortening the future, bringing the dreamer closer and closer to death; and while there is seldom a suggestion of outright fear of death, there is a distinct suggestion of the fear that it is too late, now, to do very much more of anything before the clock stops altogether. If the clock of the dream has already stopped, it may mean that the dreamer does fear death or feels that to all intents and purposes his life has already come to an end.

Coconut—Coconuts are symbolic of women's breasts by reason of their shape and contents.

Cooking Utensils—In dreams as in life, these suggest the preparation of food and are thus associated with love, warmth, and a complete home. (See Cook, Dining Room, Kitchen, Eating.)

Cradle—When a cradle or crib appears in dreams it is suggestive of the following: a dreamer who wishes he could return to the coddled security of his babyhood; a dreamer who thinks he is being treated like a baby; a dreamer who wishes to have a child; a dreamer who thinks of someone else as a child.

Should the bough break and the cradle fall, or should any similar mishap occur, the indications are that the dreamer is not too sure of the security offered by the childhood condition or whatever it is that he is currently dependent on. And if a child is snatched from the cradle the indications are that the dreamer considers himself, or someone close to him, to be a "cradle-snatcher" or "kidnaper."

Crocodile—The crocodile is a particularly nasty carrion-eating creature, and the dream-crocodile is likely to be symbolic of a particularly nasty dream thought that has emerged from the murk of the unconscious or a really loathsome impulse that has reared its ugly head. The nastiness and the loathsomeness is, of course, all in the dreamer's mind; he is revolted and frightened by his own thoughts.

Crutches—The crutch or crutches seen in dreams nearly always represent the dreamer's feelings about himself; he feels that he is a mental, moral, or other sort of cripple; or he is acknowledging that there is something in life that he is using as a crutch—liquor, pills, religious obsession, or similar prop. Sometimes the crutch repesents another individual upon whom the dreamer is too heavily dependent or even a job that he is afraid to break away from. (There are times, of course, when dream-crutches are exactly what they seem; the dreamer may have a real-life, physical need for them.) On occasion the dream-crutches may indicate the dreamer's feeling that, if only he were disabled in some way, he might be able to avoid some of his responsibilities and probably gain sympathy (love) at the same time. Suprisingly, Prince Ali comes close to agreement with the scientific dream analysts on the subject of crutches: "To dream that you are compelled to use them, denotes that you are too dependent and lack self-reliance, consequently no power to spur ahead."

Diamond—Diamonds in a dream symbolize love, or the wish for it, almost no matter how you look at them. (The "almost" is for the benefit of jewelers and diamond miners.) The diamond is a precious jewel, as is love; it is worth money, which in itself symbolizes love; and it is commonly associated with engagement rings and marriage, which are high along the road of love. Therefore to dream of a diamond or of diamonds is to dream of love—but not without a suggestion of good, solid, financial security combined with the quality of diamond-hard strength and durability.

Dice—To roll the dice is to play a game of chance. One who dreams of seeing dice or throwing them is indicating that he is uncertain about the outcome of some venture, or that he suspects himself of gambling with his life or with life's opportunities, or that he would like to take bolder chances in life and thus make greater gains, or that he feels that he is subject to the dictates of blind chance rather than his own will.

Dog—Dogs in dreams sometimes represent the animal instincts of the dreamer; when the dreamer is being threatened or attacked by a dog the likelihood is that he feels himself—or herself—attacked by the urges of his animal ego. Further, dogs are usually enemies of cats, and cats symbolize women, therefore a dog attacking a cat may be representative of a man's attack upon a woman—either a man's desire to assault and probably hurt a woman, or a woman's fear of being used/abused sexually. A dogfight in a dream is usually indicative of the dreamer's own feelings of hostility. People who are particularly fond of dogs tend to regard them, unconsciously, as human beings, and to identify very closely with them; when a man dreams of his own pet dog the probabilities are that he is actually dreaming about himself. In that case, whatever happens to the dog in his dream is symbolic of his hopes or fears for himself. (For example, if the dog is run over, the indication is that the dreamer is expressing his own death wish. But it must be borne in mind that this sort of interpretation is only valid if the dreamer really does identify with his pet. If he doesn't, then naturally another meaning must be sought.) Other dreamers regard dogs as inferior, servile creatures, and when they dream about dogs they tend to be using the dogs as symbols for people of whom they do not think very highly.

Doll—A doll in a dream may be a helpless image of the dreamer himself/herself, or it may be a representation of a "living doll" known to the dreamer. However, since dolls are made for children and are usually cast in the image of babies, most dreams of dolls have something to do with babies. They are frequently symbolic of the dreamer's desire to have a child, or of the dreamer's desire to enjoy once again the advantages of childhood, or of the dreamer's sense of acting or being treated like a child. When the dreamer is a youngster and the dream doll is "hurt" or mutilated in any way—or lost—the indications are that the young dreamer is jealous of a sibling and is venting his resentment by dream-hurting or disposing of the doll substitute.

Engine—An engine represents a driving power or force that must be skillfully controlled; an engine seen or operated in a dream usually represents the dreamer's own "drive." The dreamer's degree of control over the engine, or his reliance on someone else to control it, is the key to the dream.

Feces—A dream of feces, or defecation, suggests that the dreamer is anxious over what he considers to be an unclean activity, probably sexual activity; he may feel that he has soiled himself or his sexual partner. Or the dream symbolism may mean that the dreamer feels he has purged himself, or should purge himself, of certain attitudes and feelings that are harmful and wasteful if retained. Or the feces of the dream may symbolize something of value that the dreamer has lost, possibly money that he has wasted; just as many children regard their own waste products as something too precious and valuable to relinquish down the drain, so do some dreamers—except that they turn the image inside out and dream of their valuables in terms of waste matter.

A word, now, from Prince Ali: "To dream that you are relinquishing waste matter, or faeces, denotes a disappointment in money matters, which may inconvenience you very much." (See also Money.)

Fence—A fence (or wall, or rail) is symbolic of restraint. In some cases it may be symbolic of the restraint exercised by conscience, while in others it is representative of restraint of a less desirable sort. The dreamer may feel that he is fenced in by circumstances, that he is inhibited emotionally, that he is being restrained by some person or force from doing something that he wants to do, or that he *should* be restrained from letting loose his desires.

Fire—Fire in a dream is a representation of sexual passion and of love, of excitement, and of lust, and sometimes of blazing anger. To stamp out a fire is to try to put down one of these raging passions, and to dream of a false alarm is to indicate anxiety over a false or unnatural form of passionate expression. The glow of coals usually represents the condition of being aroused, and a blazing, all-consuming fire suggests a sexual excitement that has gotten dangerously out of bounds. To quote the sage, "To dream of fire is a happy augury, so long as you do not get burned."

Floor—The floor that we stand on in dreams seldom has much significance unless particular attention is drawn to it by the dreamer's own actions or the way he makes the floor itself behave. The floor may be considered as those principles upon which the dreamer stands; if the floor is in a bad state of repair or if the dreamer remains upright with difficulty, the indications are that he feels his own foundations to be none too steady. If the dreamer finds himself lying on the floor, the suggestion is that he feels himself to be morally degraded.

Fox—A fox in a dream often symbolizes someone regarded by the dreamer as clever and sly. That person may be the dreamer himself, in which case the emphasis is usually on "clever"; the dreamer considers himself to be a pretty sharp fellow. If the fox is symbolic of somebody else, the chances are that it is someone whom he considers to be quick-witted, inventive, but rather sneaky.

Gold—Gold, in a dream, often symbolizes something lasting and precious: a beautiful memory, perhaps, or a deep and durable love.

Gun—A gun of any sort—pistol, rifle, revolver, and so on—suggests explosions, violence, sometimes death. Its use may indicate an emotional explosion on the part of the dreamer. Quite often this explosion is sexual, because the gun is commonly employed as a symbol for the male organ. A man who dreams of using a gun may be revealing his aggressive tendencies, or his sexual desire, or simply a wish to go hunting. A woman who dreams of being shot is likely to be expressing her fear of sexual activity, for if she did not associate sex with violence she would not have selected the gun as a dream symbol. On the other hand, it is perfectly possible for a dreamer to dream of guns and to have in mind totally non-sexual thoughts about murder, target-shooting, and so on.

Hat—A hat is to the human body what a roof is to a house, and as dream symbols hat and roof usually symbolize much the same thing: the dreamer's intellectual powers or higher thinking processes—his "thinking cap." Sometimes the condition of the hat may represent the dreamer's state of mind. To some dreamers, the hat is an image of power or authority; the one who wears the hat (or uniform cap, or even crown) is the one who leads.

Horse—The horse, wouldn't you know, is a classic symbol of masculine sexuality and wild, unrestrained animal passion. If a man dreams of a horse or horses he is probably expressing his own sexual desires or some aspect of himself that he feels is powerful and possibly reckless; he may be "feeling his oats" or he may be afraid that his animal ego is going to run away with him. A woman's dream of horses may be symbolic of intercourse (astride a galloping horse), or fear of sex (chased by a horse), or wish-fear of rape (attacked or trampled by a horse). Some dreams of horses, like some dreams of guns, actually have nothing to do with sex; the context, action, and emotional tone accompanying and following the dream must all be considered in the search for other meanings.

Ice—Ice in a dream suggests that the dreamer regards himself or someone else as emotionally cold, or that he is aware of some threatening danger that looms because of his own unacceptable impulses or his inability to cope adequately with life's challenges; he is slipping, or sliding, or skating on thin ice, and he feels bound to fall. In some cases the ice may refer to the ultimate coldness, which is death.

Insects—Little plaguing thoughts appear in dreams in the guise of swarms of bugs or insects, nibbling at the dreamer and fluttering against his dream-body. When they bite, they are probably pangs of conscience; when they swarm around him persistently and defy all efforts to be brushed away they probably represent guilt or

101

anxiety obsessions. Sometimes they represent "dirty thoughts" that persist on coming back even though the dreamer does all he can to fight them off.

Jewelry—Jewels and jewelry symbolize treasure, things of great value—or a particular thing of great value that has two main aspects, one called chastity and the other called love. A young girl's dream of giving a jewel as a gift may be interpretable as her wish to give away her chastity; or it may be interpreted as an expression of love for someone upon whom she does not necessarily intend to bestow her virginity. To dream of giving or receiving dime-store jewelry is probably to dream of a poor substitute for love, of a love that is only a cheap and worthless imitation of the real thing; and to dream of exchanging really beautiful and valuable jewelry is to dream of a love of great value. More direct symbolism is carried by a ring; rings are often used in dreams to suggest the female genitals, and thus a dream of a lost ring may carry the idea of lost virginity. This may be a wish or a hope or a *fait accompli*.

Key—A key seen in a dream may represent the dreamer's desire to find a key or solution to his problems; or it may represent the dreamer's sexual desire (the key is a phallic symbol, capable of opening up objects that are employed in dreams as female sex symbols —for instance, jewelry boxes); or it may suggest the dreamer's desire to lock himself into his own inner world . . . or to free himself from it.

Knife—Knives, swords, daggers, and similar cutting objects often serve as symbols for the joint ideas of sex and violence. For those who think of sex as violent and possibly painful, or as an aggressive act, the knife is as common a symbol as a gun. In some cases the knife is a symbol of violence without sex, and in some cases it is a symbol of neither sex nor violence but rather of a severing of relationships or a figurative stab in the back.

Ladder—The appearance of a ladder in dreams usually indicates the dreamer's desire to raise himself in some way: to rise above his baser impulses, to rise above his humble beginnings, to achieve success in business, to achieve success in love, or to achieve a position of authority over others. For a dreamer to dream that someone or something is climbing up a ladder toward him is an indication that the dreamer feels anxiety or fear about something in himself or his life situation.

Lamp (Lantern, Lights)—To a dreamer of religious inclination a lamp or lantern may be indicative of spiritual light. To such a dreamer the lighted dream-lamp may be symbolic of a feeling that spiritual knowledge or insight has been achieved, or it may reveal the dreamer's wish to "see the light." For a dreamer of a different type the lamp usually represents a wish for light to be shed on a particular problem or puzzling circumstances—or an acknowledgment that light has already been shed on something that has been troubling him.

Lock—A lock in a dream suggests either some kind of security or some kind of impasse. One who dreams of trying to break open a lock may be revealing a wish to "unlock" someone's virginity, or perhaps a desire to solve a problem. If the dreamer is the victim of the lock, that is, if he is restrained by it, he is probably expressing his feeling that he is locked in by his own inhibitions or trapped by circumstance. If he uses it to secure himself in a house or room, he is indicating his need for security or his wish to keep out troublesome thoughts or ideas (by retreating into his own mind and closing it). If the

103

dreamer tries many doors and finds that he cannot open any of the locks, the indications are that he feels all doors are closed to him; that he is unwelcome beyond those doors and alone in the world. (See also Key and Locking.)

Luggage—Luggage is quite often employed in a dream as a female sexual symbol, as are many other receptacles and containers. If it is particularly burdensome it may instead be interpreted as a weight on the mind or conscience. Sometimes it is simply an accompaniment to another, more dominant symbol—that of traveling, or going on a journey. (See Traveling.)

Milk—Dreams of milk are often very similar in meaning to dreams of babies (see Baby) and are suggestive of immaturity on the part of the dreamer. If the emphasis is on the dreamer pouring milk for someone else, the suggestion then is that the dreamer *is* a mature individual who would like to provide another person with nourishment, security, and love. This, in turn, indicates either that the dreamer would like to have a child or be a mother to someone (possibly an adult love object), or that he/she would like to be the dispenser of the milk of human kindness.

Mirror—When a dreamer looks into a mirror and sees himself, that is precisely what he is doing—seeing himself. Or rather, he is looking at his alter ego, the second self embodying his repressed desires and other undesirable aspects of himself that frighten or displease him. In projecting his own image the dreamer is trying to reject that part of himself of which he disapproves. Often the image is distorted, further indicating what the dreamer thinks of the unpleasant part of himself. Sometimes there is little or no distortion, and when this is the case the suggestion is that the dreamer feels he should take an honest look at himself or take stock of what he has become.

Money—Generally speaking, money in a dream symbolizes love, although it sometimes has other meanings for some dreamers. If a dreamer dreams of giving money, the significance usually is that the dreamer is giving love; if a man dreams of giving money to a woman, the chances are that he wants to make love to her. If money is lost in the dream, or if coins are dropped, the indication is that the dreamer feels that he or she is throwing love away. If the dreamer steals money, or has it stolen from him, he may feel that he is stealing love that rightfully belongs to someone else, or that his love object has been stolen from him. If the dreamer spends his money lavishly, he may be indicating a fear that he is throwing his affections around too freely and spending too much of himself, or he may be revealing a wish to love more freely. If the dreamer saves up his money and stashes it away, the suggestion is that he feels himself unable to give love—either because of his inhibitions, his emotional immaturity, or his (feared) sexual inadequacy. If a male dreamer dreams that a woman has stolen money from him, he is probably revealing his feeling that he is sexually submissive to women. If a male dreamer feels that he has been underpaid or cheated by a short-change artist, the chances are that he feels himself to have been sexually underendowed by nature, or that he is dissatisfied with the love he is receiving in return for his own.

When a woman dreams that she is being cheated out of money, the chances are that she is dissatisfied with the love she is receiving, or that she feels she has been cheated in her sexual role—she would rather be dominant, perhaps would prefer to have been born a man. A woman who dreams of having great wealth is either expressing her satisfaction with the love she is receiving or revealing that she would like to be more sexually active and perhaps be the dominant partner.

When a dreamer dreams of having no money at all, he or she may be expressing an awareness of emotional barrenness . . . or the sad and simple fact of life that he or she actually doesn't have any money at all.

According to Freud, money in dreams frequently symbolizes feces—that precious bodily matter that children are so reluctant to relinquish. Freud pointed out a striking waking-life connection between money and feces: that the tendency to suffer from constipation often goes along with the tendency to accumulate money. Misers, in other words, tend to be constipated. They love their money and hate to let it go; they hate to let *anything* of themselves go.

Other dreams of money have yet other meanings, some of them quite direct. Dreams of picking up coins generally reveal the dreamer's yen to accumulate money (possibly for the purpose of building up a nice case of constipation); and some dreams of earning, having, spending, and losing money relate to feelings of power and superiority. Sometimes, in dreams, the payment of money has to do with the conscience, or has a religious significance: The dreamer feels that he has something to pay for, to atone for.

Monkey—Monkeys seen in a dream may be representative of "sinful" thoughts or impulses, or—since they are "so human" and often rather comical—they may be symbolic of man at his puniest and most ridiculous. Interpretation must depend on the actions in the dream and the dreamer's associations . . . and on who plays the part of the monkey.

Oil—The appearance of oil in a dream (depending on the exact nature of the appearance and how the oil is used) may indicate one of the following: the dreamer's wish to pour oil on troubled waters, or his acknowledgment to himself that some such action is required; the dreamer's feeling that some balky situation could or should be improved by the application of some figurative oil that would get things moving more smoothly or remove the friction; the dreamer's fear that something is slipping away from him; the dreamer's feeling that he is being victimized by oily or slippery characters; the dreamer's desire to be more sophisticated and cunning himself.

Oven—An oven in a dream is often symbolic of the womb, although in some dreams it may be related directly to cooking the food that symbolizes love. (It might be noted here that, even when a symbol may be interpreted in two or more different ways, the "different" meanings are not always very far apart.)

Owl—The owl is supposedly a wise old bird, and thus to some dreamers the dream owl symbolizes wisdom. To others, however, the owl is classifiable among the bats and rats and sinister animals that represent unpleasant, sometimes terrifying, thoughts.

Peach—See Cherry.

Plants—A number of plants seen in a dream, as opposed to a single tree or flower or fruit, is usually suggestive of the dreamer's own state of being. The state might be physical, spiritual, emotional, or mental; the individual dreamer will have to decide that for himself. When the plants appear to be healthy and flourishing the indication is that the dreamer feels himself to be the same; when the plants appear to be dying of drought or neglect the suggestion is that the dreamer feels some lack within himself. Plants that are growing in a state of tangled confusion are symbolic, usually, of inner confusion, while weeds growing in amongst them are probably symbolic of the dreamer's feeling that he has failed to root out whatever is objectionable within himself. Flowers that are in full bloom and trees that are loaded with fruit are suggestive of a dreamer who feels that his life is pleasant and productive.

Puppet—A puppet seen in a dream usually symbolizes the dreamer's feeling of helplessness and possibly inferiority. The puppet may be the dreamer himself, in which case the dreamer is almost certainly revealing his feeling that he is dependent on others for every move he makes and completely unable to make free choices or manage his own life; or the puppet may represent some other person, in which case the dreamer *may* be expressing contempt for somebody else but is probably expressing his wish that a strong, dominating person of his close acquaintance could be reduced to some weak and malleable creature—a figure of fun, rather than fear.

Purse—A purse is commonly employed in dreams as a female sexual symbol. As a receptacle of any sort it is in line for that position, but as a receptacle for money—love—its credentials as a sex symbol are surely unassailable.

Rabbit—It seems a little unlikely but it is nevertheless true that some people do use rabbits as dream symbols of fertility. Well, rabbits are uncommonly productive, and a dream of rabbits might very well be a wish-fulfillment dream of fertility.

Rocket—A rocket or similar missile seen in a dream is usually symbolic either of masculine virility or of the dreamer's desire to become spectacularly successful—to skyrocket to the heights of fame. If it explodes, the significance is probably sexual. (All cigar-shaped objects, particularly those containing explosive material, may be regarded as phallic symbols and often as symbols of aggression as well.)

Sausage—Serious dream analysts don't even mention sausages, for some reason; but if they did, we can guess what they would say. Confirmation of our guess comes from Prince Ali: "Sausage. To dream of making them, is a warning of excess regarding sexual appetite. To eat them, augurs love intrigues. To see them in large quantities, carnal desires."
See? Another phallic symbol.

Scales—These, in a dream, represent justice and balance. The dreamer is likely to be expressing his feeling that he is, in some way and for some particular deed or attitude, being weighed in the balance. (In a sense, the scales are his conscience.) The other details of the dream, and the dreamer's own associations, are needed for an explanation of exactly what is being weighed and what "justice" may be expected on the basis of the weighing.

Scissors—The use of a pair of scissors in a dream suggests that the dreamer wishes to cut his way through something, possibly red tape; that he wishes to separate himself from someone else or form a particular situation; that he wishes to separate himself from life; or that he feels hostile toward someone and would like to hurt or kill him.

Skyscraper—Was anybody in any doubt? Male sex symbol.

Snake—The snake is quite commonly employed as a symbol of the male organ or of sexual desire. A dream including a snake is not, however, necessarily a "sex dream," even though it may have sexual connotations. Snakes symbolize not only sexual virility but original sin, evil lust, temptation, and cunning. Thus a dream that features the killing of a snake may be interpreted as a successful battle against evil or temptation—of *any* kind, the sexual kind included. Some snake dreams, of course, have nothing whatsoever to do with sex, as witness scientist Kekulé's revelation regarding the benzene ring.

Snow—Snow seen in a dream may indicate that the dreamer is feeling lonely and depressed, or emotionally cold. On the other hand, to some dreamers snow may be symbolic of purity and cleanliness, and to such dreamers a dream of snow may be indicative of a feeling of self-satisfaction or serenity, or of a wish to be, once again, "as pure as driven snow." The snow, or something snowy-white, may also be a symbol of abstract purity, or the quality of purity attributed by the dreamer to another person. Thus to sully the snow is to commit an impure act or to soil someone else. Dreamers who dream of being snug and warm inside while it is cold and snowy outside may be dream-gratifying a desire to return to the cozy, warm, and secure days when they were well insulated from the cold outside world.

Soap—The appearance of soap in a dream usually indicates guilt feelings on the part of the dreamer and his wish to cleanse himself by washing away some real or imagined sin.

Toilet—A dream of a toilet suggests the dreamer's need to purge himself of some attitude or habit that he feels is wasteful or poison-producing. Possibly he has become aware of something within himself that ought to be eliminated—something "poisonous" such as hatred, hostility, and so on. To a dreamer who regards sex as "dirty," or no more than a bathroom function, or who has guilt feelings regarding a particular sexual relationship, the use of the toilet may be symbolic of the sex act.

Tomato—If seen alone or in bushel baskets, probably no more than an edible fruit; if seen in pairs, symbolic of a woman and specifically of the female breasts.

Trash—The appearance of trash or garbage in a dream suggests the dreamer's feeling that he has associated himself with something worthless and shoddy, that he regards himself (probably temporarily) as trashy and soiled, that he feels his surroundings are ugly and sordid, or that he regards someone else as a cheap and trashy individual. The throwing out of trash usually indicates the dreamer's feeling that he has inner garbage to dispose of.

Tree—A tree in a dream frequently symbolizes fertility, procreation, and life itself. It may also be symbolic of the family tree—that is, of the parents and even the ancestors. If a dreamer dreams of a fallen tree, that tree is usually himself; and if the dream tree flourishes the indication is that the dreamer is himself asserting the creative principle.

Umbrella—The umbrella is sometimes employed as a phallic symbol and sometimes as a shield against the storms of life. Interpretation depends on the context, individual associations, and emotional coloring of the dream.

Vampire—Vampires, vampire bats, or other creatures that cling tenaciously and suck the blood are not uncommon figures of the nightmarish dream. The dreamer who suffers one of these creatures may be indicating his feeling that someone or something is sucking him dry and weakening him emotionally or physically; or he may be revealing his awareness that one of his own clinging habits or attitudes has a firm and destructive hold on him.

Veil—When a veil appears in a dream the indications are that the dreamer has a desire to hide some forbidden thought or impulse, or that he feels that others are concealing something. Usually, when the veil is lifted, the indications are that the dreamer has become aware of some important truth, probably about himself. The nature of the truth will only become apparent when the dreamer, upon waking, probes his own mind very carefully.

Water—Water, as something that flows from a faucet or fountain into a tumbler or tub, is usually indicative of the water of life. It comes from what might be called the font of life and may be regarded as the principle of life itself. To drink it is to be spiritually or emotionally nourished, and thus a dream of drinking water may express the dreamer's wish to refresh his spirit. To wash in it is to be cleansed and purified, and thus a dream of washing in the flowing water is suggestive of the dreamer's wish to wash away his sins and purify himself.

Window (Windshield)—A window is a breakable barrier, and thus a common symbol for the female sex organ. Thus, when a woman dreams of someone breaking in through her window she is probably dreaming of the sex act, or, more specifically, of defloration; and when a man dreams of climbing in through a window, *he* is probably dreaming of the sex act. If he dreams of climbing in at a window and stealing jewels, he is almost certainly dreaming of sexual intercourse. In other dreams a window may simply be something through which the dreamer looks out upon the world; what he sees outside is more important than the window. If a dreamer should open the dream-window from the inside, he may be expressing a wish to find some outlet for his impulses.

Yardstick (Ruler, Measuring Tape)—"To see a yardstick in your dreams denotes that your exacting ways are disliked by others and on this account are often shunned." That's the way the old-time dream books would explain the yardstick symbol, and there may be an element of truth in what they say. A dream of measuring something very meticulously and with exaggerated care indicates a dreamer who may be so finicky about details that he irritates other people. It is more likely, though, that a dreamer who uses a yardstick or other measuring device is either expressing doubts about measuring up to his own or other set standards, or that he is taking someone else's measure . . . thus expressing subtle doubts about that other person.

SIX

Happenings:
Doing or Being Done

The dreamer is usually doing something in a dream, or participating in some happening, or having things happen to him. Sometimes he seems to be a disembodied observer, but more often he is part of the action and moving it along in some way. He is capable, in dreams, of doing things that he cannot do in everyday life— things such as floating and flying and perching atop enormously tall, swaying ladders without toppling off . . . or falling from a tremendous height and landing like a feather. He is also capable of running through the streets stark naked without being arrested, and sometimes without even being noticed.

These rather spectacular dreams are fairly common. That is, they are experienced every once in a while by a great many dreamers; they are "typical" dreams. This does not mean, however, that these dreams occur to all of us with any great frequency. For the most part we get around in our dreams very much as we get around in daily life—by walking, or driving, or riding the buses. Even these actions are usually underplayed unless they have significance in a dream. If the point of the night tale lies in how fast we run to catch the train or how hard we have to paddle to get upstream or how well we drive the car, then the dream points up these details.

But if it doesn't really matter how we get from place to place, we just find ourselves there. Dream "action" doesn't consist only of locomotion or mere physical action. It consists of happenings: things that we cause to happen, things that happen to us, exciting natural occurrences, action situations in which we find ourselves.

Of course, nothing really happens to us; we make it happen, whether "it" is an earthquake or our own murder. Why do we create these strange situations for ourselves? Why do we permit someone to hurt us when, after all, it is our dream, and we should be able to plot as pleasant a course as we please? Because we have ideas to express and needs to fulfill; because we have wishes to gratify and guilt feelings to punish.

And when you feel the least bit guilty in the dream . . . when you have the slightest feeling that you deserve to be punished . . . Pow! the dream punishes you; you are part of a happening. You asked for it, you got it.

Now it's up to you to figure out *why* you asked for it.

Adultery—Most dreams of adultery apparently star someone other than the dreamer, because if the dreamer has adulterous thoughts on his mind he tries to disguise them in some way. Thus, very often, a dream of someone else's infidelity is a projection of the dreamer's own infidelity or unfaithful thoughts. By projecting, he protects himself from unpleasant self-knowledge and manages at the same time to pass the buck: if the other party is guilty, then what the dreamer is actually doing himself can't be so bad after all. Sometimes a dream of another person's adultery is expressive of the dreamer's feeling that the other person has betrayed him in some way, perhaps by actually committing adultery or by being unfaithful to an ideal or a memory. And some dreams of adultery are open admissions of the dreamer's desire for extra-marital relations.

115

Arguing—An argument with an individual who is portrayed literally in the dream is strong evidence of a genuine conflict with that individual. (In a certain "savage" society, such a dream would prompt the dreamer to go to his antagonist upon waking and straighten things out in advance, so that there would be no quarrel. It's not a bad idea for sophisticated societies, either.) More often, a dream argument is indicative of inner conflict; the antagonistic ideas warring within the individual start shouting at each other. Each participant in the quarrel is an aspect of the dreamer himself, an idea or impulse that is in contradiction with the other aspects. Sometimes, when there are only two participants in the argument, one of them represents the dreamer's conscience. In fact, even when a group quarrel is in progress, one of the voices can nearly always be identified with the conscience—or the "good" impulses.

Bathing—Most dreams of bathing, not surprisingly, have something to do with cleansing. A dream of bathing or washing suggests guilt feelings on the part of the dreamer and an acknowledgment by him that he could use some sort of moral or mental purification. To some dreamers the dip into water is a direct equivalent of baptism; to them the need is for moral cleansing and spiritual rededication. To others, the idea of being able to wash away one's sins is an appealing wishful thought; washing may be a superior kind of "white-washing" that actually washes away or annuls the shameful act or urge, permitting the dreamer to feel that it never occurred. In some cases, taking a bath might have erotic significance, especially if the dreamer shares the tub with someone else.

Bleeding—Blood in a dream is a common but complex symbol, usually associated with injury, hostility, sex, or the monthly cycle. What is important in a dream of blood or bleeding is who did what to whom, whether the dreamer is a man or a woman, and the mental hangover left by the dream—fear, revulsion, relief, guilt, or whatever. If a dreamer sees blood flowing in a slaughterhouse or butcher shop, the indications are that he is harboring deep rage and hostility. A man who dreams of seeing another man bleeding from a wound is suggesting his hostility toward that individual, and possibly a castration wish for him as well. This, in its turn, may mean that the dreamer is jealous of that individual and/or that he is in conflict about his own masculinity. If the dreamer sees himself bleeding because of self-inflicted injury, the chances are that he feels a need to punish himself for some urge or action. If the dreamer sees himself bleeding because of the actions of others, he is suggesting his feelings of being unwanted, abused, and possibly threatened by others. When a woman dreams of hurting a man to the point where blood flows, the chances are that she is expressing her wish that he might be emasculated, a wish that is probably rooted in jealousy or fear of him. Sometimes a woman's dreams of blood or bleeding refer to her own monthly cycle and may be (depending on the context) expressions of her wish for, or fear of, pregnancy. And quite often a dream in which blood appears may be interpreted as having reference to defloration, especially when the blood appears as a spreading stain across a snowy surface. Many such dreams refer to a very early, and significant, sexual experience.

Burning—A fire burning in a dream suggests hot temper, sexual passion, destruction, or even a high fever (as when the dreamer is lying in his sickbed, "burning up"). A dreamer who sets the fire and enjoys the blaze is probably expressing his desire to free himself from his inhibitions and let his sexual passions go ahead and blaze. If he sees it burning and feels that he wants to put it out but cannot, the suggestion is either that there's nothing he can do about it now except let it run its course, or that he feels something in his life is being destroyed (his hopes are going up in smoke) and he is powerless to prevent it. Or he may feel that there is a situation in which he would like to get involved, but that he had better not take the chance of getting his fingers burned. If the dreamer is distressed by the fire and/or makes an active attempt to fight it, he is probably expressing a wish to control either his anger or his sexual urge. And, of course, something burning may relate to a real-life circumstance.

Burying (Being Buried)—When a dreamer dreams of burying someone it usually symbolizes his death-wish for that person or his acknowledgment that "love is dead" or a relationship has ended. When the dreamer sees himself being buried, he is probably expressing the idea that he is overwhelmed by his problems, that he would be better off dead, or that he deserves to be punished (death being the ultimate punishment) for his misdeeds or "sinful" urges. Dreams of being buried alive are indicative of great anxiety.

Changing Into Another Person—This is not so much a dream action as one of the mechanisms of the dream world. When one person changes into another, and then perhaps into yet another, what is happening is that one particular quality or set of qualities is being expressed first by one person who happens to possess that quality, and then by another, and then by another. It is quite possible that not one of these individuals is actually the person he appears to be, but each one of them possesses a quality characteristic of—or highly reminiscent of—the

118

individual about whom the dreamer is really dreaming. Thus the apparent metamorphosis of one person into another is hardly a change at all—it is merely a change of masks, or symbols. The same surface change can be seen in settings and objects; they may change their looks or change their shape but their essence remains unchanged.

Cheating—Someone who dreams of cheating in an examination or a card game is likely to be expressing one of the following thoughts: a wish or acknowledgment of being unfaithful; fear that his chosen (love or business) partner is cheating on him; a feeling of insecurity, of inability to pass life's tests without relying on hypocrisy, insincerity, lies, flattery, undercover deals, or some other form of cheating; or a feeling that the only way one can make out in the world of today is by being more conniving than the other fellow.

Choking—A dream in which the dreamer experiences the sensation of choking suggests that the dreamer feels he actually is being choked in some way, either by some physical condition or by some undesirable, anxiety-causing impulses. Sometimes feelings of guilt cause a conscience reaction which demands punishment in this unpleasant form. When a person dreams of choking someone else he is either choking himself (again as punishment) or expressing feelings of extreme hostility toward an individual or life in general.

Choosing (Making a Choice)—There are many dream situations in which the dreamer feels called upon to make a choice of some kind: going or staying, taking the left fork in the road or the right, choosing one course of action over another. Such dreams represent conflict situations in the dreamer's life and can usually be interpreted quite easily in the light of the dreamer's waking knowledge. To marry or not? To take the job or to go on to college? To be part of the "establishment," or strike out on his own course? The dreamer alone knows what his real choices are.

Climbing—A dream of climbing a mountain or a stairway may be indicative of the dreamer's ambition, of his desire to reach the heights of business or social success. Just as often, the act of climbing to the heights—and descending from them—is symbolic of sexual intercourse. Failure to reach the top may indicate the dreamer's sense of personal failure or his inability to achieve sexual satisfaction. Success—well, interpretation depends on the details surrounding the dream-climb and the dreamer's own associations.

Cooking—To cook, in a dream, usually means to give love and comfort to another. This often holds true even when the cook-dreamer actually does spend much of his or her waking time in cooking for others. Interpretation must depend largely on the details of cooking and serving. If the person doing the cooking (and the dreaming) is unable to prepare a palatable meal or does not actually serve it, the indications are that the dreamer feels incapable of giving love. If the dreamer dreams of someone else doing the cooking and then failing to serve the meal, the chances are that he feels disappointed in the love that he hoped to receive. If the dream-cook serves a delicious meal and nobody wants to eat it, he/she probably feels unappreciated and unloved. If the dreamer dreams of being provided with delicious food but in minute quantities, the indication is that he feels he is getting love in small and sparing doses; he is being tantalized by tidbits. And so on and so on. . . . The combinations and interpretations are not too difficult to figure out.

Crying—Crying, in a dream, may be indicative of a feeling of fear or sorrow or general despondency, or it may be a hypocritical camouflage for pleasure feelings that the dreamer knows to be inappropriate.

Cutting—The significance of cutting something in a dream depends very much (although by no means altogether) on what is cut. Cutting string or cloth or paper, for instance, may be symbolic of one of the following: the dreamer's desire or intention to sever all ties with someone or something; the dreamer's awareness of the desirability of detaching himself totally from a situation or giving up certain long-cherished ideas (almost certainly self-destructive ones); the dreamer's awareness that it is high time he cut the umbilical cord, or the apron strings; the dreamer's fear that he is being separated from someone or something that has been dear to him. A dream of cutting down trees may indicate the dreamer's fear of getting the axe, or being cut down by somebody; or it may indicate his wish to chop down (reduce) somebody else. A dream of cutting off a branch, a human limb, or part of a plant is suggestive of the castration complex—a wish for castration for someone else, coupled with fear on the part of the dreamer. Or it may indicate the desire to cause injury and pain. (See Injury.)

Dancing—Dreams of dancing almost invariably have sexual connotations. In fact, dream-dances are usually indicative of a wish for sexual intercourse with the dream partner or whoever is symbolized by that partner.

Dreaming of Dreaming—Most dreamers, once in a while, will have a dream about dreaming, waking up, thinking about the dream or something else—only to wake up some time later and realize that the first waking was part of the dream. The dream within a dream is a device employed by many of us dreamers to reduce reality to fantasy. If we can turn a difficult real-life problem into an unreal or fantasy situation by dreaming of it, we have in effect nullified it; something that is "only a dream," or a product of our imagination, is obviously not real. At least, that is what we dream-think.

Drinking (Being Drunk)—Drinking, in dreams, usually has reference to the joys of babyhood, particularly when the liquid concerned is milk or an alcoholic beverage. One who drinks in a dream is likely to be expressing a yearning to be mothered or otherwise relieved of the responsibilities of adulthood; or he is revealing a feeling of helplessness and dependency; or he is feeling lonesome and would like to share in the juvenile conviviality characteristics of a bar or soda fountain. Sometimes one who dreams of drinking—without particularly caring what he is drinking—may actually be thirsty. In this case the dream serves the dual function of wish-fulfillment and guardian of sleep. If the dreamer does not satisfy his genuine thirst with a dream-drink, he will probably wake up to do so. When a dream character, either the dreamer or someone else, appears to be drunk, the suggestion is that that character is as helpless and dependent as a baby. When a dream character who is ordinarily symbolic of an authority figure or moral force (judge, captain, policeman, and so on) is seen to be drunk in the dream, the indication is that the dreamer is doing a bit of rationalizing: If the "moral force" is a helpless drunk he isn't very much of an authority, and anyway he is incapable of exerting himself. Therefore the anti-moral impulses are free to go about their merry way. (See also Bar, Bartender, Drunkard.)

Driving—One who dreams of himself as driving a car or other vehicle is revealing at least a degree of belief in his own qualities of mastery and independence. He may not drive well, but at least he is driving instead of being driven to a destination chosen by another. If he drives skillfully and in the right direction, the indications are that he is healthily self-confident. If he drives so badly as to have a collision, the suggestion is that he does not have his own impulses under sufficient control and is afraid that these "drives" are going to get out of hand. The worse the collision, the greater his fear of being overwhelmed by those wild impulses. Sometimes, if speed is the cause of the crash, it may mean that the dream-driver is aware of the dangers inherent in his habit of making hasty decisions. If the driver is frustrated at every turn by one-way signs (pointing in the wrong direction), or roadblocks, or a string of red lights and stop signs and markers that say "Detour," "No Turns," and "Road Closed," the inference is that he feels his life or some major effort or course of action to be thoroughly futile. (See Automobile, Driver, Passenger.)

Drowning—A dream of drowning may be symbolic of the dreamer's feeling that he is overwhelmed by circumstances or inner problems—that he is going under. Or it may be interpreted in terms of a return to infancy, spiritual rebirth, or death. (See Water, Bodies of.) A dream of someone else drowning is strongly suggestive of the dreamer's hostile attitude toward that person. If a dream-stranger drowns, or several people drown, or if the dreamer dreams of a particular place where people have supposedly drowned, it is possible that there are things the dreamer would like to forget: Perhaps he wants to drown his memories.

Dying (Death)—When someone dreams of dying he may be revealing a wish to die or a need to punish himself (rather severely) for something that he has done or perhaps only thought about doing: He may be so disgusted by his secret thoughts and inner, almost uncontrollable urges that he feels he deserves to die. (Having thus punished himself by a dream-death, he usually feels better in the morning.) In some cases a dream of dying is indicative of the dreamer's wish to join a departed loved one. This is particularly likely to be true if the departed loved one actually appears in the dream.

A dream of the death of a loved one who is not really dead at all is indicative of the dreamer's death-wish for that person. The love is nonetheless genuine, even though it is complicated by a kind of instinctual sexual rivalry. In this kind of dream the victims of the death wish are more likely to be parents than mates; quite often a girl or grown woman will dream of her mother's death so as to reduce the competition for the father's affections, and quite often a man will dream of the death of his father so that he might have his mother to himself. Awake, these dreamers are quite unaware of their hidden hostilities and quite convinced of their love for both parents.

To dream of *anyone's* death may represent a murderous impulse, or an acknowledgment that there is no longer any significant emotional value to the relationship. Love itself is dead. Similarly, a dream in which a dead person appears to be alive is an indication that the departed one has come alive again emotionally, or has never really died in the dreamer's heart.

Sometimes a dream of someone else's death is a kind

of defensive move on the part of the dreamer. One who loves very much may sometimes also fear very much—fear that the loved one will suffer, or fear that the loved one will abandon them by dying. Thus the dream operates as a sort of emotional safety valve, permitting a preview of the tragedy and an escape for some of the emotional reaction to it. In a way it softens the blow that may eventually come, and partly immunizes the dreamer to the real-life tragedy. Dreams of this sort are quite common when the dreamer is very dependent on the individual upon whom the death dream is based, especially if that individual is already ill. When the tragedy does actually occur in real life—perhaps many years later—the dreamer has, through his dreams, already expended some of the emotional energies that otherwise would have been expended at the crisis time. These energies are more easily, less painfully, expended during sleep. As a device, it is quite effective in lowering the intensity of genuine, waking sorrow, and may actually permit the bereaved one to maintain a degree of composure that might otherwise have been lacking.

One final note on dreams of death: They do not always appear to *be* dreams of death. A dream of someone who is dead or may die does not necessarily feature that person. What the dream is like and what it does contain depends on what the dreamer feels about death. The symbolism used in the dream may be an empty chair or room, an undelivered letter, a broken telephone connection, or a cold and ancient creature staring the dreamer in the face. Or it might even be the wide, free ocean or a vision of paradise.

Earthquake—Dreams of earthquakes sometimes indicate that the dreamer feels he is going to explode or suffer some kind of breakdown—or simply that he needs to let off steam. Sometimes dreams of earthquakes are expressive of the sex act. For some reason, far more women than men employ this particular sex symbol.

Eating—Eating, in a dream, is usually associated with love. Sometimes, eating a meal with someone is actually a symbol of intercourse; and sometimes the business of eating may represent the dreamer's desire to make someone or something a part of himself. If the meal suddenly disgusts him, then the indication is that the object of his desires is in some way prohibited (either because of the dreamer's religion, his upbringing, social standards, or something of the sort).

Otherwise, the quality of the food and the service is usually the key to the dream. If the dreamer doesn't enjoy what he is eating, the chances are that he is not too happy in his love life. If he eats great quantities of food, whether tasty or not, the indication is that he feels emotionally starved. If an enormous amount of food is thrust upon him, he may feel that *he* is being devoured by someone else's unwelcome and voracious love. And so on. . . . (See Cannibal, Cook, Cooking.)

Falling—Dreams of falling are nearly always accompanied by dream feelings of great anxiety. The dreamer often finds himself teetering atop a high, swaying ladder or hanging onto the edge of a cliff; his heart flutters, his feet slide, his hands slip, his equilibrium is going, going, gone—! Dream falling actually is indicative of a loss of mental equilibrium, which in waking life may manifest itself in loss of self-control, loss of temper, or a moral lapse. Thus, a person who dreams of falling may be expressing doubts about keeping his temper or other emotions in check. Quite often, when a woman dreams of falling, she is expressing the idea (and probably fear) of yielding to sexual temptation. In some cases the dream fall may be indicative of some sort of fall from grace: loss of esteem in the eyes of a loved one, loss of the boss's esteem and consequent loss of job prestige, or a loss of society's acceptance because of undesirable behavior. A dream in which someone else falls may be indicative of the dreamer's death-wish for that person.

Fighting—Dreams of fighting with another person or being engaged in a battle express the aggression deep within the dreamer. Whether he is the aggressor or the victim, and whether he fights with weapons or with words, the dream-fighter reveals by his dream that he is carrying on a war with himself or with other people. He may even be carrying on a war with the world; if he dreams often of aggressive encounters he is probably expressing his feeling that the world is full of ugliness and conflict.

Floods, Flooding—A flood is the result of something that is uncontrolled. Either Nature has gone on a rampage or the bathtub faucet has been left to run. Thus a dream of seeing a flood or being overwhelmed by one is usually symbolic of the dreamer's feeling that his emotions are getting out of hand. Even an overflowing bathtub or kitchen sink may be suggestive of uncontrolled emotions, and a rising tide of floodwater may very well be the dreamer's warning to himself that it is time to head for higher and drier land or he is likely to be engulfed.

Flying—There are many possible interpretations of the flying dream, and it may as well be said at once that one of them is sexual. Freud is chief among those who have said that dream-flying may be expressive of the act of intercourse. He also said that flying dreams (which he himself had never experienced) may be an attempt to

127

recapture the pleasant, swinging and rocking sensations of infancy and early childhood. Thus the dream-flight may be a wishful return to the happy, carefree days of early youth and the games of movement that provided such pleasurable "genital stimulations." Another interpretation, probably rare in application, is that flying may be a symbol of death. This may be the case when the dream-flier hovers in the air like a disembodied spirit looking down detachedly upon the world beneath.

For other dreamers, the dream-flight may be indicative of a desire to rise above certain problems or find freedom from unpleasant, earthbound situations; and for some, a dream of flying over the heads of other people may be a symbolic expression of the desire to dominate others or "put them in their place."

Forgetting, Being Forgotten—Dreams in which the dreamer forgets something, loses something, or accidentally leaves somebody behind are indicative of the dreamer's wish to obliterate a thought, get rid of the object, or free himself from that person. The individual who is accidentally-deliberately left behind may be very much loved by the dreamer in real life, but for a well-hidden reason the dreamer feels an equally well-hidden resentment toward him . . . until the dream uncovers the secret. The cause of the resentment may be discovered in other details of the dream, or perhaps in other dreams.

When the dreamer himself is left behind, or dreams of being lost, the probabilities are that he feels lonely and abandoned. He may feel that people literally want him to "get lost," or that they have "forgotten" him somewhere because they don't want him. A dream of this type is particularly common among dreamers who were, or thought they were, neglected in their childhood.

Gambling—One who dreams of gambling may be suggesting to himself that he is taking unwarranted chances with something in his life, possibly his personal relationships, his career, or even his health. Or he may be revealing that he thinks of himself as weak—as a person who does not or cannot make his own choices and guide his own life but instead relies on chance to nudge him here and there on an unplanned course toward a future that may or may not have its rewards.

Gardening—A dream of gardening usually suggests that the dreamer would like to create something, and in most cases the "something" is human life. More often than not there are two people in the dream garden, suggesting the dreamer's acknowledgment that it takes two to bring a new life out of the garden. (See also Garden, Gardener.)

Graduation—Graduation represents the twin concepts of preliminary achievement and transition to a more advanced stage of life. Thus, one who dreams of graduating is likely to be expressing a feeling that he has successfully negotiated the preparatory phase of life and is now ready to take the next step up. The dream may have reference to a first job, a promotion, leaving home for the first time, or possibly impending marriage.

Illness—One who dreams of being ill may be expressing fears for his own health, an awareness that there already is something wrong with him, a desire to be coddled, or guilt feelings leading to a wish for self-punishment. Or he may be wishing for illness to give himself an excuse for not doing something that he doesn't want to do. One who dreams that someone else is ill may be expressing concern for that person's welfare, but is more likely to be indicating feelings of resentment and hostility.

Imprisonment—A dream of being imprisoned is usually indicative of the dreamer's feeling that he is locked into himself, or trapped by some real-life circumstance, or that he should be restrained from indulging his wilder impulses, or that he should be punished for something he has already done. A dream of someone else's imprisonment is suggestive of the dreamer's feeling that another person deserves to be punished or restrained; or of his desire to prevent someone from "getting away" from him. (See also Convict, Prison.)

Inability to Act/Move—Among the most typical of the typical dreams is the one in which the dreamer is rooted to the spot. He wants to move forward, or leap onto the train, or run from a pursuer, or at least cry out, but he cannot; his limbs and his vocal cords are paralyzed, and the only movement is the pumping of his heart. His inhibition of movement is indicative of the inhibition of an impulse by a contradictory impulse: The dreamer wants to go but at the same time he wants to stay; he wants to reach out for something, but a different something is holding him back. The "impulse" involved is very often sexual in nature, and may be either the impelling force or the inhibitory force. If it is the impelling force, the dreamer feels that he would like to chase after it but is frustrated by the moral inhibition that says—"Hold it right here!" If it is the inhibitory force, the dreamer's strong inclinations are to escape the impulse that threatens to overtake him (usually her), but is glued to the spot by a frightening but compelling wish to give in to that impulse. Women, particularly, have this kind of dream; the dreamer feels extremely anxious and would like desperately to make a get-away (to run from the forbidden experience), but finds to her horror that she cannot move and that the male pursuer is almost upon

130

her (that the experience *is* going to occur). Resolution of the problem is so difficult that, nearly always, the dreamer can only solve it by awakening.

In some cases, a dream of being glued to the spot may represent the dreamer's awareness of some self-created impediment to his progress through life: possibly laziness, or poor work habits, improper diet, or over-indulgence in alcohol. He isn't getting anywhere because he has put obstacles in his own path; he will be able to get somewhere when he himself removes them.

Injury—A dream of being injured may be symbolic of guilt feelings and a wish for punishment, or it may be suggestive of a feeling of inadequacy. One who dreams of losing a limb by accident or surgical amputation is likely to be expressing the idea of emasculation: In a way he would like to be a woman, but at the same time he would like to be an adequate masculine figure. Sometimes dreams of injuries or wounds are indicative of defloration, of some sexual episode that occurred way back in the dreamer's past. If a woman dreams of being wounded or of losing a limb, she is likely to be expressing sexual jealousy or indicating that she feels "hurt" by circumstance or another person.

Laughing—Laughing in a dream is actually no laughing matter. Though there are, of course, exceptions, the chances are that the laughing dreamer has his mind on a situation that is difficult and unfunny, and is attempting to minimize the problem by pretending that it is ridiculous. He is laughing with tears in his eyes. (See also Laughter.)

Lightning—Lightning, in real life, is a great, natural burst of electrical energy that seems to take over the viewer's very being. It is not altogether different in the dream. The dream bolt may be representative of a surge of sexual energy, or of a sudden, inspirational idea or insight. Or it may be indicative of the dreamer's hope of being enlightened in respect to some distressing problem.

Locking Up, Locking Out—A dream of locking up someone, including the self, suggests the dreamer's awareness of the need for self-control. (See Imprisonment and other related categories.) However, locking up the house may be indicative of the dreamer's wish to seal himself off from the unpleasantness of the outside world, or it may be an indication of his need for security. In some cases, closing and locking all doors from the inside may suggest the dreamer's awareness of certain negative attitudes that repel other people and thus leave the dreamer to his own lonely resources.

Misfortune—There are all kinds of misfortunes that occur in dreams, and their nature (thus, also, their interpretation) varies from dreamer to dreamer. But one thing can be said for certain: There are no accidents in dreams. If the happening is in the dream it is put there by the dreamer, and thus it is no accident. Nearly all dream misfortunes serve a dual purpose: First, the collision or natural disaster (or whatever it may be) represents the dreamer's feeling that he is riding for a fall or is about to go off the rails unless he holds himself in check; second, the misfortune is a form of self-punishment for whatever excess the dreamer suspects himself to be guilty of. Quite often, the dream-punishment is out of proportion to the suspected crime. Hardened criminals do not feel guilty, as a rule, while people of high moral and ethical standards tend to punish themselves for every minor lapse.

Missing a Train (or Other Vehicle)—Dreams in which the dreamer runs for and misses a train or other moving vehicle are all, naturally enough, dreams about failure to catch up with something. A frequent interpretation of what is known as the coming-too-late dream is that the dreamer doesn't really want to catch the train because, deep down, he is fully aware that he is trying to chase after an improper or neurotic goal that he *knows* is impossible to attain. Much as in the inability-to-move dream, the dreamer is caught between two contradictory desires and usually winds up with nothing. If he has a really compelling desire to catch that train, and if he knows the goal is acceptable, he can usually make the extra effort required to leap aboard. ("Missing" is an accident, which as we know does not exist in dreams.) Sometimes the dreamer who misses his train is revealing a compelling desire *not* to achieve a certain goal or do a particular thing; he is telling himself that he tried, but the truth of it probably is that he is going out of his way to avoid doing whatever it is that is symbolized by the train. In dream terms, he could have caught it if he had really wanted to; in real-life terms, he hasn't been trying.

Other dreams of missing a train may be indicative of lost opportunity. A dreamer of almost any age may dream of challenges unanswered, of opportunities that have slipped away, of the fact that "it is later than you think." Quite often, when elderly people dream of missing a train, they are expressing their feeling that life is passing them by; essentially, they would like to recapture their youth but are aware that they cannot. Occasionally, when youngsters dream of missing trains, they are revealing a childish desire to "catch up"—in age, schooling, or parental affections—with an older brother or sister.

And once in a while a missing-a-train dream may be

indicative of a real case of fatigue on the part of the dreamer. If he feels too weary to catch that dream-train, it is quite possible that he is also too weary to catch a real-life train. The dream could be his means of acknowledging that he is nearing a state of exhaustion and had better take care of himself.

Murder—Much of what is said about Death, Dying, Corpses, Dead Persons and so on also holds true of dreams about Murder. One important additional point should, however, be made: When the dreamer feels, in real life, that he loves someone too much or that the object of his love loves *him* too much, he tends to feel a need to reduce or overcome that love or else be over-whelmed by it. He cannot overcome it, however, and in dreams he knows it; it is so strong that his only recourse is to kill the object of his love. Dreams of murdering a parent may often be similarly explained. The youngster —or even a grown-up son or daughter—feels uneasy about his/her over-attachment to the parent, and blames the parent for his own feelings. A very loving son may thus dream of murdering his mother, when what he is really trying to do is keep his own love for her within the bounds of normalcy.

Naked (or Almost) in the Street—Dreams of walking around in various stages of nudity are so common that they necessarily have a multiplicity of explanations. The simplest is that the dreamer feels ashamed of some-thing, thus strips himself bare of all pretense. In a sense, he is also exposing himself to the criticism he feels he deserves. Practically the opposite interpretation may also be true: A dream of disrobing may be indicative of the dreamer's desire to strip away the restrictions im-posed by society's standards of morality and live a more free-wheeling life. However, shame, rather than a sense of freedom, is the more usual accompaniment to dreams of nakedness. Some dreamers even exhibit a touch of masochism by having the dream onlookers stare and point while the naked one searches desperately for a place to hide. That he cannot find a hiding place is, of course, no accident; he wants people to cluck indignantly and send for the police. A dream of this sort is usually indicative of the dreamer's guilt feeling or possibly his inferiority complex: He bares his weaknesses, he invites criticism, he suffers from the stings of scorn, and he is able to tell himself that he has every reason to be ashamed. The onlooker's contempt is actually his own.

The Freudian interpretation of the "exhibition" dream is that it is expressive of the infantile exhibitionist desire that lies not quite dormant within the hearts of all of us. Nobody, it seems, is totally without the desire to flaunt his nakedness, and since it is difficult to get away with this in real life except under rather special circumstances we use the dream as a wish-fulfillment device. At the core of this wish is the desire to recapture one's early childhood days when nakedness was permissible and even cute, and the conflicts of life were few and simple. The criticism of the onlookers is probably suggestive of the dreamer's awareness that it is impossible to return to the innocence of childhood. When the dream-nude is ignored by the passersby, which he often is, the chances are that he has succeeded, in his dream world, in recapturing briefly a little of what has been lost. Or else the dreamer may feel that he is fated to be ignored no matter what he does.

One who dreams such dreams is *not* an exhibitionist. Waking-life exhibitionists tend to dream of the nakedness of others.

Reproaching (Being Reproached)—When the dreamer reproaches someone, or is himself reproached, he is almost certainly reproaching himself and thus expressing feelings of guilt.

Riding—Dreams of riding a bicycle may be interpreted in much the same manner as dreams of driving a car, with a little additional emphasis on sexuality because of the manner of propelling a bike. Dreams of riding a horse, however, are nearly always totally sexual. (See Horse.)

Running—Dreams in which the dreamer finds himself running are occasionally indicative of his desire to reach some goal and reach it quickly. More often, though, a running dream is accompanied by the fear and the notion of a pursuing figure, in which case the dreamer is likely to be revealing his fear of being overtaken by his own disturbing impulses or a situation that he regards as threatening. If the dream-runner freezes in his tracks as the danger closes in on him, the indications are that he is torn by an inner conflict. (See Inability to Act/Move.)

Searching—A dream in which the dreamer is searching high and low for something or somebody is usually indicative of his desire to find an answer to a problem. He may not, consciously, even be aware of the problem, but how he goes about his search and what he actually finds in the dream should help to reveal its nature—and possibly its solution—to his waking mind.

Shooting—If a dreamer dreams of shooting or being shot he is probably expressing his view of sex as violent and dangerous. Either that, or he is looking forward to the opening of the hunting season. (It is no joke to suggest that these two views are not entirely incompatible.)

Soiling, Being Soiled—To soil something is, of course, to dirty it, and thus to dream of soiling or being soiled is to dream of degradation. Usually the significance is sexual, and often the reference is to defloration.

Stealing—Stealing is a crime, and one crime in the dreamworld is quite often substituted for another. If the dreamer dreams that he has committed the crime of theft he *may* be revealing his feeling that he has taken something that does not belong to him, but in all likelihood he is telling himself that he has done something else that is "wrong." The misdeed may consist of an antisocial act, the violation of a religious taboo, or a sexual transgression. In a sense, no matter what the crime, the dream-criminal *is taking*—taking too great a liberty, taking a life, taking a love that is forbidden, and so on. If the dreamer dreams of someone else doing the stealing, he is either suggesting that he regards the other person as a criminal or that the other person is stealing his love from him. If the latter, the dreamer probably has a love-hate attitude toward the other person; he loves and resents at the same time, and pretends that his own excessive love is the other person's "fault."

Storm—A storm brewing and breaking is usually representative of the dreamer's inner turmoil. It may be sexual; it may not be. Whatever it is, it is quite violent and in need of release.

Swimming—Swimming is a sensual and pleasant activity, and swimming dreams are often symbolic of another sensual and pleasant activity. . . . Swimming with somebody else is *quite* a sexy dream. In some cases, the dream swim may be suggestive of a wish to return to the warmth and comfort of the womb, and may thus be described as a conception fantasy. In other cases, a dream of swimming—particularly in a river—is suggestive of movement and progress, either in business or love or idealistic strivings. The difficulty or ease of the swim, the emotions accompanying it, and its successful or unsuccessful completion are all clues in the interpretation of it.

Tearing—Whatever is torn in a dream is often symbolic of human flesh, thus one who dreams of tearing something is likely to be dreaming of hurting someone else. The nature of the intended injury is usually castration or defloration, and the dream is probably derived from fear and envy in the case of the first and guilt feelings in the case of the second. If a dreamer dreams that something about himself—some item of clothing, for instance—is being torn, he is probably indicating a desire to hurt himself based on his guilt feelings for hating or wanting to hurt somebody else. If a woman dreams that her dress has been or is being torn, she is probably recalling her introduction to sex or expressing her fear of the sex act.

Teeth Falling Out—Once again we encounter the familiar castration (for the self or another) wish, with its overtones of guilt and fear, but we also have a number of promising alternatives. The first and most direct is that a loss-of-teeth dream is a pointed message from the dreamer to the dreamer that his teeth have been neglected and he had better go and see his dentist. Another is that a dream of loose teeth is suggestive of loose talk, and that falling-out-teeth is suggestive of very loose talk indeed—running off at the mouth, so to speak. For some dreamers, a dream of losing teeth is symbolic

138

of growing old; if this is the valid interpretation, the chances are that the dream is colored by anxiety and sadness.

If a tooth appears to be rotten and the dreamer manages to get rid of it without apparently feeling pain, then there will probably be no accompanying feeling of anxiety—because the significance of the loss is probably the successful solution of a problem, an amicable but much-desired divorce, or recovery from an illness.

"Getting rid of a person," as in the case of divorce, is quite often a valid interpretation of the loss-of-teeth dream. A whole mouthful falling out may be indicative of anxiety and tension (and possibly even night grinding) rather than hostility, but a single tooth falling from its place is strongly suggestive of a single family member leaving the group. Thus, the loss-of-tooth dream may be a "get-lost" wish for a parent, mate, sister, brother, in-law, or other relative.

Traveling—To dream of traveling or going on a journey is to dream of the journey of life itself. The journey represents the life force or the impulse to live . . . although for some the journey may be coming to an end. Usually a dream of traveling suggests that the dreamer feels he is on the move and going places; if others go off and leave him behind the suggestion is that he feels he is getting nowhere.

Urinating—Sometimes a dream of urinating is intended as a prod to the dreamer to get up and go to the toilet, but probably more often it is symbolic of the dreamer's feeling that there are "poisons" within himself that should be expelled; he feels guilty of harboring envy, malice, hatred, wayward impulses or unpleasant thoughts, and he would like to purge himself of them.

Warning—A warning in a dream may be delivered by the dreamer himself, by another character, or even someone apparently returned from the dead; but whoever delivers the message and whoever gets it, the warning is intended for the dreamer himself and nearly always represents his own conscience. ("Don't do it—it's wrong! Be careful!" "Control yourself!" "If you don't study you'll fail!") Nonverbal warnings are also to be found in dreams, although they must be scrutinized very carefully because they usually have other interpretations as well. For instance, a dream of failing brakes followed by a collision may indicate a loss of emotional control, but it should also be taken as a reminder to have those brakes checked before they really fail and involve the dreamer in a waking-life encounter with another object.

Wedding—A dream of a beautiful wedding is all that it may seem: It is either a preview of the planned event, or a wishful glimpse into a hoped-for future. However, if the wedding is postponed or canceled, or if the bridegroom doesn't show up, the indications are that the dreamer is still in two minds about having to grow up and leave home. She (men very seldom dream of weddings) may truly love the groom but she is not altogether sure that she is ready to step into a strange new life.

If the wedding seems to go as planned but the wedding gown is torn or soiled, the indications are that the dreamer is not bringing her full quota of chastity with her to the occasion or that she regards marriage in terms of degrading sexual relations.

SEVEN

Emotions, Sensations, and Various Intangibles

The following conceptions consist of dream aspects that would be intangible even if they were real—that is, that *are* intangible even in waking life. But let us not forget that these are by no means the only abstractions presented in dreams; nearly all abstract ideas in the dreamer's mind are presented in the form of people, creatures, places, or things, and we have therefore met most of them already. The following brief list consists simply of some of the dream elements that resist standard classification.

Such dream symbols as youth, air, various colors, clouds, or numbers need little more explanation than appears in the appropriate paragraph. Emotions, though, may require somewhat more thought. The very important emotions of love and hate are barely mentioned in this section, largely because they tend to be represented in the dream by other symbols and partly because they are so complex as to defy any effort to pin them down. The least of their complexity is that one may appear in the guise of the other; we all know that love and hate go hand in hand—which may be the basis for the old saw that dreams go by opposites—but, in knowing that, we don't know nearly enough. When something about a relationship, no matter how passionate it may be (or perhaps because of its intensity), makes it slightly revolting to the dreamer, he is able to transform that real-life emotion into its dream opposite. "Too much" love may express itself in violent hatred, sometimes culminating—as we have seen—in murder. But we cannot generalize from that that dream hatred is necessarily indicative of too much love; feelings of hatred or self-hatred may be due to entirely different reasons. Much the same can be said of desire and fear. These are also hand-in-glove opposites, and they are not simple, either, but there is mention of them on a later page because they do help to illustrate the principle of bipolarity—and to show that it doesn't always hold true. (See Anxiety, Fear.)

The emotional content of the dream is extremely important, though it can obviously be misleading. The emotion experienced is likely to be responding to the real meaning of the dream rather than to its symbolism or apparent content, and if it at first seems misplaced or inappropriate that is because we do not yet understand what the dream is really about. We have to weigh all symbol meanings very carefully. When there is no apparent emotion, we must look for it; if there is too much emotion, or if it seems not to fit the dream, then we must look into it. But we must never overlook it.

Age—Not surprisingly, the actual age of the dreamer has much to do with interpretation of dreams in which the dreamer is conscious of himself as being old or young. When youth dreams of youth the significance is probably minimal, but when the middle-aged or elderly dream of being young they are probably expressing one of the following thoughts: that they feel as vital, exuberant, and forward-moving as they did in their youth, or that they wish they still had their youthful strength and vitality in order to more successfully accomplish their middle-age projects, or that they wish they could be young and carefree again . . . with all of life still to be lived.

If a youthful or immature dreamer dreams of being old he is likely to be expressing the wish to grow up so that he can enjoy adult privileges or telling himself that it is time he started behaving in a more mature manner. If an adult dreams of being very much older than he is, he may be expressing a wish for death, a fear of death, or a desire for the presumed wisdom and serenity of old age. Or he may simply be thinking wishfully of a time when he can retire and rest upon his laurels (which would probably tend to age him very rapidly).

Air—Rare indeed is a dream about air that's just *there* and not doing anything, but if such a phenomenon is encountered it may be symbolic of the breath of life, without which we wouldn't be doing any dreaming or anything else at all. Slightly more common is a dream in which the air around the head is in a state of turmoil; this may be indicative of a mind in a similar state. More common yet is a dream feeling of being suspended in air —neither flying, floating, soaring, or falling, but just being there—which is probably symbolic of the dreamer's feeling that he is indulging in fantasies instead of having his feet planted firmly on the ground. A dream feeling of lacking sufficient air to breathe comfortably is probably indicative of an anxiety state with its accompanying respiratory difficulties.

Anger—Anger in a dream is usually a reflection of the dreamer's own waking attitude. Even if the anger is expressed by someone else it tends to be the dreamer's own emotion. He is probably hostile, aggressive, angry with the world and particularly with himself, and ready to bubble over with violence. However, the anger in a dream, even while being genuine self-anger, may be the accompaniment or even a kind of cover-up for a totally different feeling—that of excessive love for, and over-dependence on, another person. The excessive love breeds a kind of fear and resentment which becomes hatred which expresses itself as violent anger—ostensibly directed at the love object or somebody else, but actually turned in upon itself. In some cases, the anger expressed in a dream may simply be the dreamer's reminder to himself to curb his temper.

Anxiety—When a dreamer feels a sense of anxiety in a dream, he is usually experiencing exactly that. There is probably something in his life that makes him genuinely anxious, or he has a touch of that anxiety neurosis so common in this tangled world of ours. But even when the anxiety is genuine, it may be (as above) precipitated by an entirely different emotion and it may serve as a camouflage for that emotion. Usually it is the precipitation or surface manifestation of a desire that the dreamer regards as forbidden: He wants something desperately, he is sure that it is wrong, he turns his desire and his conflict into anxiety.

Clouds—Clouds are about as ephemeral and desultory as anything we are likely to encounter in a dream. Whatever their nature—heavy and stormy, wispy and delicate—they are at the mercy of the weather system and the winds. A dreamer who dreams often of seeing drifting clouds is likely to be revealing his feeling that he himself has no direction but that which is given to him by the winds of chance. The chances are that he is not a person who easily makes his own decisions but rather permits himself to be nudged here and there by others.

Colors—Despite those analysts who profess to see no significance in dream colors, there are many others who detect in them the expression of emotions or perceptions. Thus, some people tend to see bright and cheerful colors in many of their dreams, revealing their general attitude that the world isn't a bad place after all; while others see things in dreary colors and drab tones, suggesting their own depression and the viewpoint that the world is grim and dreary. Black, in a dream, suggests a really bleak outlook on life, perhaps even that it is a living death, and white is suggestive of innocence and chastity. Something white that has been soiled by another color, usually brown or red, is suggestive of a loss of chastity. Red is indicative of blood, love, and immorality, and blue may be used as a symbol of piety or sadness. Green, as in waking life, may be used to express envy, and yellow is often indicative of cowardice. Of course, any color may have associations with something in real life, and must therefore be scrutinized in the light of the dreamer's own recollections.

Despair—A feeling of deep despair or despondency in a dream is usually indicative of a serious real-life problem. The dream is often an attempt to solve that problem in a perhaps drastic way, for example, the "accidental" death of another individual. The despair continues, then, because the dreamer knows he still has the problem and now he has compounded it with a feeling of guilt. Sometimes, the feeling of despair is what is known as a "rehearsal-reaction" to some terrible thing that the dreamer rather hopes will happen—for example again, that someone close to him will die and thus permit him to "mourn" the loss for which he secretly hopes.

Disappearance—When somebody who has been playing a part in a dream suddenly and unaccountably disappears, it is probably because the dreamer would like that person to vanish or get lost.

Fear—Fear is to desire what love is to hate; it is its other face. To fear something in a dream is often to want it very much, and at the same time to be frightened by the intensity of the desire. There are exceptions: In some dreams the dreamer is expressing a fear of retribution for some real or imagined misdeed, and the fear is at the same time a cover-up for his guilt feelings and a form of self-punishment. (See also Missing a Train, Running, Inability to Act/Move.)

Happiness—Happy dreams, or feelings of happiness in dreams, are usually indicative of the general well-being and serenity of the dreamer. However, if these dreams are unrealistically rosy and consistently tell the dreamer how marvelous he is, how admired, how successful, how handsome, and how sought-after, then there is a very strong likelihood that the dreamer is unhappy in waking life and produces wish-fulfillment dreams to make up for reality.

Laughter—Laughter in a dream may occasionally be due to a truly comical situation or a funny line, or even to a bubbling-over of real happiness, but more often than not it is the result of an insight that the dreamer doesn't really want to have, or accept. The laughter makes a difficult situation or realization bearable; it covers up the sadness. When a dreamer regards a dream situation as funny and laughable, the chances are that he has put his finger on a very basic conflict. Seeing it, essentially understanding it, he cannot face it, and so he

146

tries to reduce the sad situation to a comic one by laughing at it.

Numbers—Dream-numbers are eagerly latched upon by addicts of the numbers game, but only in the rare and totally coincidental case have they actually paid off. Numbers do have a significance in dreams, but that significance has nothing to do with luck. It has to do with the facts of the dreamer's life. In a way, dream-numbers when frequently employed may tell a kind of story; they may refer to dates which have a secret importance for the dreamer, or they may have to do with people's ages, or the size of a group, or the number of children the dreamer has, or the number of months or years ago that he did a particular thing, and so on and so on. The dreamer himself has to bring his memory and ingenuity to bear on the puzzle of decoding numbers in the dream. Some numbers, particularly 1, 3, and 0, have—because of their shape—a certain sexual symbolism, but it is impossible to even hazard a guess as to when this interpretation may apply without knowing the context of the dream, the emotional coloring, and the dreamer's associations.

Pain—Pain in a dream, though it may sometimes be a carry-over from waking life, is usually a substitute for something else—either another physical sensation, or a painful problem. The physical sensation that it most frequently represents is that of sexual gratification. Thus the dream-pain may be the dreamer's camouflaged reenactment of a pleasurable but forbidden experience, and at the same time express the dreamer's need for self-punishment. It may even be his reminder to himself that he had better not try to repeat the experience, or he will suffer for it. In other cases the pain may be representative of the dreamer's inner conflict in regard to some life problem of personal weakness. He may suffer the pain himself, or he may displace it to another person in order to make it bearable. Occasionally, one who suffers pain in real life is similarly able, in a dream, to displace it or project it to another person, thus achieving a measure of relief.

Past—Most dreams relate, one way or another, to the past, but if a dreamer persistently dreams of returning to an earlier stage of his life he is attempting what is known as annulment of time. If he repeatedly dreams of being a youngster again, that is probably exactly what he wants to be; if he is married in real life and dreams of being a young bachelor, the chances are that he is having frequent second thoughts about his choice of marriage partner—or simply that he does not particularly enjoy the responsibilities of marriage and would like to postpone them to some indefinite future.

Surprise—If a dreamer feels a sense of surprise in a dream it is probably because he has become aware of something about himself that had escaped him before. Thus he is either wondering at the strangeness of his own thoughts, or he is wondering at an insight he has achieved about himself. He is having a—"Well, how about that!"—reaction to something he has seen in his own dreaming mind . . . a reaction which is extremely common when any dreamer, upon waking, collects his dream thoughts and starts to sort them out.

"...extraordinary...literally staggering...
one of the most powerful books I have ever read...."
—RICHARD KLUGER, EDITOR, New York Herald Tribune Book Week

THE
PAINTED
BIRD

Jerzy Kosinski

95037/95ᶜ

If your bookseller does not have this title, you may
order it by sending retail price, plus 15¢ for mailing
and handling to: MAIL SERVICE DEPARTMENT,
POCKET BOOKS, A Division of Simon & Schuster,
Inc., 1 West 39th St., New York, N.Y. 10018. Not
responsible for orders containing cash. Please send
check or money order.

PUBLISHED BY
POCKET BOOKS
(A 5/9)

A Merriam-Webster

REG U S PAT OFF

THE LEADING NAME IN DICTIONARIES SINCE 1847

REG U.S. PAT OFF

The New
MERRIAM-WEBSTER
POCKET
DICTIONARY

This 640 page pocket-size dictionary has been specially prepared for general use by the recognized leading dictionary makers.

MORE THAN 42,000 VOCABULARY ENTRIES

GUIDES TO SPELLING AND PRONUNCIATION

SELECTED ETYMOLOGIES GIVING PRECISE WORD HISTORIES

SYNONYMS

COMMONLY USED ABBREVIATIONS

FOREIGN WORDS AND PHRASES

POPULATION FIGURES FOR THE UNITED STATES AND CANADA

75320 / 75¢